3-MINUTE
DEVOTIONS
FOR WOMEN

JOURNAL

Published by Barbour Books, an imprint of Barbour Publishing, Inc., 1810 Barbour Drive, Uhrichsville, Ohio 44683, www.barbourbooks.com

Our mission is to inspire the world with the life-changing message of the Bible.

Member of the
Evangelical Christian
Publishers Association

Printed in China.

3-MINUTE DEVOTIONS

FOR WOMEN

JOURNAL

BARBOUR BOOKS
An Imprint of Barbour Publishing, Inc.

INTRODUCTION

Most days we're seeking out a moment or two of inspiration and encouragement—a fresh breath of air for the lungs and soul.

Here is a collection of moments from the true Source of all inspiration and encouragement—God's Word. Within these pages you'll be guided through just-right-size readings that you can experience in as few as three minutes:

Minute 1: Reflect on God's Word

Minute 2: Read real-life application and encouragement

Minute 3: Pray

These devotions aren't meant to be a replacement for digging deep into the scriptures or for personal, in-depth quiet time. Instead, consider them a perfect jump-start to help you form a habit of spending time with God every day. Or add them to the time you're already spending with Him. Share these moments with friends, family, coworkers, and others you come in contact with every day. They're looking for inspiration and encouragement too.

Your word is a lamp to guide my feet and a light for my path.
PSALM 119:105 NLT

HE ENJOYS YOU

"The LORD your God is with you, the Mighty Warrior who saves.
He will take great delight in you; in his love he will no longer
rebuke you, but will rejoice over you with singing."

ZEPHANIAH 3:17 NIV

Memory is a powerful part of each one of us. Perhaps you can see your father cheering you on in a sports event, or you remember your mother stroking your feverish forehead while you lay sick in bed. With these mental pictures comes a recollection of emotion—how good it felt to be cheered and encouraged—how comforting it was to be loved and attended.

Zephaniah's words remind us that God is our loving parent. Our mighty Savior offers us a personal relationship, loving and rejoicing over us, His children, glad that we live and move in Him. He is the Lord of the universe, and yet He will quiet our restless hearts and minds with His tender love. He delights in our lives and celebrates our union with Him. We can rest in His affirmation and love, no matter what circumstances surround us.

Lord, help me remember that You are always with me and
that You delight in me. Remind me that I am Your child
and that You enjoy our relationship. Amen.

I must Remember I can do anything- God is With me At all Times. When my patience wears thin I try to think of Jesus and That helps so much!

SWEET AROMA

The heartfelt counsel of a friend is as sweet as perfume and incense.
PROVERBS 27:9 NLT

When you think of the word *comfort*, what comes to mind? Maybe it's a favorite pair of jeans or a well-worn sweatshirt. It might be chocolate or homemade mac and cheese—foods that soothe in a difficult time. Or perhaps it's a luxurious bubble bath, complete with candles and relaxing music.

While all these things can bring temporary relief, God's Word tells us that finding true comfort is as simple as sharing heart-to-heart conversation with a friend. Whether it's over coffee, dessert, or even on the phone, a cherished friend can offer the encouragement and God-directed counsel we all need from time to time.

Friendships that have Christ as their center are wonderful relationships blessed by the Father. Through the timely, godly advice these friends offer, God speaks to us, showering us with comfort that is as sweet as perfume and incense. So what are you waiting for? Make a date with a friend and share the sweet aroma of Jesus!

Jesus, Your friendship means the world to me. I value the close friendships You've blessed me with too! Thank You for the special women in my life. Show me every day how to be a blessing to them, just as they are to me. Amen.

Friend ARe wonderful!
You only need one Vary
close friend to Confide
it. Its A must to
Talk and release the
stresses.

FULL OF GRACE

*Let your conversation be always full of grace, seasoned
with salt, so that you may know how to answer everyone.*

COLOSSIANS 4:6 NIV

Inflection. Tone of voice. Attitude. Maybe you remember your mom saying, "It's not what you say, but how you say it." Words not only convey a message, they also reveal the attitude of our hearts. When our conversation is full of grace, even difficult truths can be communicated effectively. But how do we season our words with grace?

Grace is undeserved favor that extends unconditional love to another. Whether you're communicating with friends, family, or coworkers, it's important to show that you value them. Put their needs above your own. Communicate truth within the context of love. Show compassion and forgiveness. Demonstrate understanding and an openness to receive their input. Respect their opinion. Rather than striving to drive home your point, try to understand theirs. Seek to build them up. Convey encouragement and hope. Be positive.

When our conversations are full of grace, people will enjoy communicating with us. They will walk away blessed by the love we have shown. Today, in your conversations, extend God's grace to those hungry to experience His love.

*Dear Lord, may I view each conversation as an opportunity to
extend Your grace to others. May my words be a blessing. Amen.*

A PROSPEROUS SOUL

*Beloved, I wish above all things that thou mayest
prosper and be in health, even as thy soul prospereth.*
3 JOHN 1:2 KJV

Twenty-first-century women do everything conceivable to keep their bodies and minds in good shape. They work out, watch their calories and carbs, and take excellent care of their skin and teeth. On the outside, many women appear to be in excellent health. But what about their souls? What would it profit a woman to be completely fit on the outside and have a sin-sick soul?

Maybe you're one of those women who thrive on staying in shape. Perhaps you even put your external body on the front burner of your life, paying particular attention to diet, exercise, and appearance. As you think about your overall health, consider your soul. Have you given your heart and life to the Lord Jesus Christ? If so, are you spending time with Him? Praying? Reading His Word? These things are necessary for a healthy soul.

Today's scripture is so encouraging. God wants us to prosper and loves for us to be in good health, even as our souls prosper. If we really think about that, we have to conclude that the health of our soul is even more important than our physical health. Spend some time today giving your soul a workout.

*Lord, sometimes I pay more attention to the outside than the inside.
I care more about what people can see than what they can't. Today I
draw near to You. Make me healthy. . .from the inside out. Amen.*

LEAD, FOLLOW, AND BLESS

*You go before me and follow me. You place
your hand of blessing on my head.*
PSALM 139:5 NLT

A kindergarten teacher explained the rules to her new students. "When we walk down the hall," she said, "I will always go first, and you must not pass me." Immediately the children asked why. She told them she would be their guide to help them know which way to go. She added that it would help her keep track of them. "I don't want to tell your parents that I lost you when they come for you!" she teased. *The teacher would go before her students.*

The admiral of a ship took a crew of Navy recruits on board. He covered standard procedures of the ship. "If the ship goes down," he said, "get the life rafts and save yourselves. I will come behind you. Once I know that all of you are safe, I will follow." *The captain would follow his sailors.*

A young mother tucked her daughter into bed. The child mumbled sleepily, "Mommy, why do you put your hand on my head before you leave my room?" The smiling mother answered, "I place my hand on your head as I pray for you, sweetie. I ask God's blessings on you as you sleep." *The mother placed her hand upon the head of her child.*

God is all three. *He leads you. He follows you. He places a hand of blessing upon you.* An omnipresent Father has you in His care.

God, thank You that You lead me, have my back, and bless me daily. Amen.

BETWEEN MIRACLES

*Then the L*ORD *said to Moses, "I will rain down bread from heaven for you."*
EXODUS 16:4 NIV

By the moaning and groaning, you'd never know that the Israelites had just been miraculously freed from slavery. They knew firsthand of Pharaoh's hard heart and had witnessed horrifying plagues that tortured their enemies. And yet, days later, when they were stuck in the desert, they doubted God's faithfulness. They wondered if God had forgotten them and if they would starve. God's answer? Another miracle. This time He rained down bread from heaven. A tangible, daily reminder that He would continue to provide for the Israelites, in spite of their lack of faith.

Have you ever experienced a miracle? A job offer in just the nick of time? An unexpected check in the mail? It's easy to praise God in the face of answered prayer and miraculous provision. We readily acknowledge His work and praise Him for His faithfulness. But all too soon, we feel stuck in the desert and wonder what on earth God is up to. Is He listening? Has He forgotten us completely? Somewhere in our distant memory is a miracle, but sometimes we just want to cry, "What have You done for me lately?"

Circumstances change. God does not. The next time you're stuck in the desert between miracles, remember the manna.

Father, how sorry I am that I forget Your faithfulness,
in spite of Your continuing provision for me. Help me
to remember and help me to be grateful. Amen.

....

....

....

....

....

....

....

SELF-EXAMINATION

Let us examine our ways and test them, and let us return to the LORD.
LAMENTATIONS 3:40 NIV

What if you could follow yourself around for the day, carefully examining all that you do? Look at your schedule—your choice of activities, the people you talk to, the things you listen to and watch, the habits being formed, the thoughts you think. Maybe your heart desires intimacy with God, but a real day in your life leaves no time for solitude. God often speaks to us in still and silent spaces. How will we hear Him if we're never still?

Taking time to reflect, to think, and to examine oneself is a necessary step in moving toward intimacy with God. Before we can turn back to Him, we must repent of the things that moved us away from Him in the first place. As we set aside time for solitude and reflection, the Holy Spirit will gently show us these things if we ask. He will show us the sins we need to confess and give us the grace of repentance. Experiencing forgiveness, our fellowship with our heavenly Father is restored.

Lord, help me to still myself before You and be willing to examine my ways. Speak to me through Your Holy Spirit of what is wrong in my life. Give me the gift of repentance, and allow me to extend forgiveness to those around me. Amen.

A HOLY LONGING

*As the deer pants for streams of water, so my
soul pants for you, my God. My soul thirsts for God,
for the living God. When can I go and meet with God?*
PSALM 42:1–2 NIV

When you think of the word *longing*, what images come to mind? We long for so many things, don't we? We long for someone to love us, to tell us how special we are. We long for financial peace. We long for a great job, the perfect place to live, and even the ideal friends.

God's greatest desire is that we long for Him. Today's scripture presents a pretty clear image. We should be hungering and thirsting after God. When we've been away from Him, even for a short time, our souls should pant for Him.

If we were completely honest with ourselves, we'd have to admit that our earthly longings usually supersede our longing for God. Sure, we enjoy our worship time, but we don't really come into it with the depth of longing referred to in this scripture. Ask God to give you His perspective on longing. He knows what it means to long for someone, after all. His longing for you was so great that He gave His only Son on a cross to be near you.

*Father, my earthly longings usually get in the way
of my spiritual ones. Draw me into Your presence, God.
Reignite my longing for You. Amen.*

WALKING IN GOD-CONFIDENCE

*If my people, who are called by my name, will humble themselves
and pray and seek my face...then will I hear from heaven,
and I will forgive their sin and will heal their land.*

2 CHRONICLES 7:14 NIV

Some people consider humility a weakness. Others think humility means never talking about yourself or always putting yourself and your accomplishments down. Christians often confuse humility with low self-esteem, believing we should not think of ourselves as worthy, because Jesus Christ was the only perfect person.

But when we accept Christ as our Lord and Savior, His life becomes ours. We are no longer slaves to sin, but we own His righteousness. So we don't have to go around thinking that we're scum. Since God reconciled us to Himself through Jesus' sacrifice on the cross, we can live each day with the confidence of knowing we're forgiven.

Our Savior walked in total God-confidence—knowing that His steps were planned—and He had only to listen to His Father's heartbeat to know which way to go. He could withstand insults, persecutions, and dimwitted disciples because He knew who He was and where He was headed.

Today, humble yourself in front of God and ask His forgiveness for the ways you've sinned. Accept His forgiveness and live in total God-confidence, knowing that He has heard you. Then you'll be able to withstand the pressures life throws at you, because He is your life.

*Father God, I praise You for Your forgiveness and healing.
Thank You that I am called by Your name. Amen.*

....

....

....

....

....

....

HIS PERFECT STRENGTH

*"My grace is sufficient for you, for my power is made perfect
in weakness." Therefore I will boast all the more gladly
about my weaknesses, so that Christ's power may rest on me.*

2 CORINTHIANS 12:9 NIV

How do you define stress? Perhaps you feel it when the car doesn't start or the toilet backs up or the line is too long at the grocery store. Or maybe your source of stress is a terrible diagnosis, a late-night phone call, a demanding boss, or a broken relationship. It's probably a combination of all these things. You might be able to cope with one of them, but when several are bearing down at once, stress is the inevitable result.

It has been said that stress results when our perceived demands exceed our perceived resources. When the hours required to meet a deadline at work (demand) exceed the number of hours we have available (resources), we get stressed. The most important word in this definition is *perceived*. When it comes to stress, people have a tendency to do two things. One, they magnify the demand ("I will *never* be able to get this done") and two, they fail to consider all of their resources. For the child of God, this includes His mighty strength, which remains long after ours is gone.

In an uncertain world, it is difficult to say few things for sure. But no matter what life throws our way, we can be confident in this: Our demands will *never* exceed God's vast resources.

*Strong and mighty heavenly Father, thank You that in my
weakness I can always rely on Your perfect strength. Amen.*

UNCHAINED!

The Spirit you received does not make you slaves,
so that you live in fear again; rather the Spirit you
received brought about your adoption to sonship.
And by him we cry, "Abba, Father."

ROMANS 8:15 NIV

Imagine how difficult life would be inside prison walls. No sunlight. No freedom to go where you wanted when you wanted. Just a dreary, dark existence, locked away in a place you did not choose with no way of escape.

Most of us can't even imagine such restrictions. As Christians we have complete freedom through Jesus Christ, our Lord and Savior. No limitations. No chains.

Ironically, many of us build our own walls and choose our own chains. When we give ourselves over to fear, we're deliberately entering a prison the Lord never intended for us. We don't always do it willfully. In fact, we often find ourselves behind bars after the fact, wondering how we got there.

Do you struggle with fear? Do you feel it binding you with its invisible chains? If so, then there's good news. Through Jesus, you have received the Spirit of sonship. A son (or daughter) of the most-high God has nothing to fear. Knowing you've been set free is enough to make you cry, "Abba, Father!" in praise. Today, acknowledge your fears to the Lord. He will loose your chains and set you free.

Lord, thank You that You are the great chain-breaker!
I don't have to live in fear. I am Your child, Your daughter,
and You are my Daddy-God! Amen.

....

....

....

....

....

....

LIFE'S DISTRACTIONS

And when they had found him, they said unto him, All men seek
for thee. And he said unto them, Let us go into the next towns,
that I may preach there also: for therefore came I forth.

MARK 1:37–38 KJV

The Sunday school director approached a young woman in the hallway. "I know you're capable of leading the high school department. You're not serving in any capacity at this time. Won't you consider the position?" The young woman felt cornered. Her gift was not teaching, and she dreaded the prospect of Sunday mornings with teenagers. Yet there was an opening, and she'd feel guilty if she didn't help out the church leader. What to do?

In Jesus' ministry, He was called upon to heal the sick and speak to the multitudes. Yet despite the clamor of the crowds, He knew His purpose. Instead of getting sidetracked and following the people's agenda, Jesus knew His priority was prayer and recognizing God's will. He never allowed people's demands to distract Him from His calling.

God designed us for a special purpose. Using our gifts is what we're called to do. When we step into a situation He didn't design for us, we're being disobedient. Filling a position just because there is an opening is never a good idea. We need to find our gifts and use them for God's glory.

Lord, point me on the path You would have me follow.
Keep me from becoming distracted. Amen.

BODY AND SPIRIT

Don't you know that you yourselves are God's
temple and that God's Spirit dwells in your midst?
1 CORINTHIANS 3:16 NIV

Amy fell into bed with a moan. She'd been on her feet all day for her retail job, and she felt old and tired.

I need to start exercising, she thought for the hundredth time that week. Every Monday, she resolved to take better care of her body, but by Tuesday she had fallen back into old bad habits. *Why do I do this?* she wondered. *Lord, help me!*

The next day, Amy called a friend to ask if she'd help keep her accountable in her exercise. "I want to change," Amy said. "But I need encouragement."

Our physical shells house the very spirit of God, and God created our bodies, so we are called to be good stewards of them. It's hard with our modern, busy lifestyle to make health a priority, but we can ask God for wisdom and discipline. After all, if He asks us to do something, He will equip us for the task.

Do you treat your body as a temple of God? What habits do you have that could change? Perhaps you could drink less soda, eat more fruits and veggies, or get more exercise. Do you smoke? Resolve to quit. Do you work at a desk all day? Get some fresh air during your lunchtime. Your body and your spirit will thank you!

Lord, give me the discipline to make wise choices about what
I drink and eat. And help me to make exercise a priority. Amen.

....

....

....

....

....

....

....

....

I AM A FRIEND OF GOD

When Jesus saw their faith, he said,
"Friend, your sins are forgiven."
LUKE 5:20 NIV

Friendships are vital to women, and godly friendships are the best. Can you even imagine a world without your girlfriends in it? Impossible! Who would you share your hopes and dreams with? Your goals and aspirations? Oh, what a blessing women of God are! They breathe hope and life into us when we need it most. They laugh along with us at chick flicks. They cry with us when our hearts are broken.

Isn't it amazing to realize God calls us His friend? He reaches out to us with a friendship that goes above and beyond the very best the world has to offer. Best of all, He's not the sort of friend who loses touch or forgets to call. He's always there. And while your earthly friends might do a good job of comforting you when you're down, their brand of comfort doesn't even begin to compare with the Lord's. He knows just what to say when things go wrong, and knows how to throw an amazing celebration when things go well for you.

Today, thank the Lord—not just for salvation, not just for the work He's done in your heart, not just for the people and things He's placed in your life—but for calling you His friend.

Oh Lord, I'm so blessed to be called Your friend!
You're the best one I'll ever have. Thank You for the kind
of friendship that supersedes all boundaries. Amen.

. . . .

. . . .

. . . .

. . . .

. . . .

. . . .

. . . .

HE IS YOUR CONFIDENCE

For the LORD shall be thy confidence,
and will keep thy foot from being taken.

PROVERBS 3:26 KJV

Sometimes we wish for more confidence. A job interview or a social situation we are facing may make us nervous. A new situation we're thrown into may cause us to worry. Will we be dressed appropriately? Will we know what to say?

Those are the times to remember that the Lord is always with us. He has promised never to leave or forsake us. He tells us we are His little lambs and He is our great Shepherd. He upholds us with His righteous right hand. He leads us along still waters and restores our soul. These are just a few of God's promises regarding the care He provides for His children.

The next time you need some confidence, instead of worrying or trying to muster it up on your own, seek God. Read 2 Corinthians 12:9 and remember that in your weakness, God shows up to be your strength. He will be your confidence.

God, be my confidence when this world brings situations
in which I feel insecure or inadequate. Thank You. Amen.

SHINING LIGHT

*"You are the light of the world.
A town built on a hill cannot be hidden."*
MATTHEW 5:14 NIV

Jesus' disciples knew all about darkness. Centuries before electricity had been harnessed to provide light, individuals made do with fires and oil lamps. When the sun went down, darkness ruled.

So when Jesus told His followers that they are the light of the world, the image meant a great deal to them. Light that overtakes the darkness—light to illuminate the way to the Savior. What an amazing concept!

Jesus tells us twenty-first-century followers to be light too, boldly and unashamedly flooding the darkness that surrounds us. How do we do it? First, by living the life God calls us to—not sinless, but forgiven. Second, by sprinkling our conversations with evidence of our faith. Did something good happen? Share that blessing with others and give God the credit for it. When someone asks about the peace they see in you, share the joy of Jesus.

Being a light of the world is not about being a Bible thumper or bashing others over the head with religion. It's about living out genuine faith that allows Christ's light to break through our everyday lives. With that goal in mind, shine!

*Jesus, You are my true light. Even though I alone can't
shine as brightly as You, I ask that You shine through
me as I seek to follow after You. I know I won't be perfect,
but I also know that Your grace has me covered. Amen.*

PEOPLE PLEASER VS. GOD PLEASER

*We are not trying to please people
but God, who tests our hearts.*

1 THESSALONIANS 2:4 NIV

Much of what we say and do stems from our desire to be accepted by others. We strive to make a certain impression, to shed the best light possible on ourselves. Wanting to be viewed as successful, we may decide to exaggerate, embellish, or even lie. It's difficult to be true to ourselves when we care so much about the acceptance and opinions of others. Impression management is hard work, so it's good to know God has a better plan!

Rather than being driven by the opinions of others, strive to live your life for God alone and to please Him above all else. God knows our hearts. He perceives things as they truly are. We cannot fool Him. When we allow ourselves to be real before Him, it doesn't matter what others think. If the God of the universe has accepted us, then who cares about someone else's opinion?

It is impossible to please both God and man. We must make a choice. Man looks at the outward appearance, but God looks at the heart. Align your heart with His. Let go of impression management that focuses on outward appearance. Receive God's unconditional love, and enjoy the freedom to be yourself before Him!

*Dear Lord, may I live for You alone.
Help me transition from a people
pleaser to a God pleaser. Amen.*

SURROUNDED BY HIS PRESENCE

Then a cloud covered the tent of the congregation,
and the glory of the LORD filled the tabernacle.
EXODUS 40:34 KJV

God wants us to enter worship with a heart prepared to actually meet Him. He longs for us to come into the frame of mind where we're not just singing about Him, we're truly worshipping Him with every fiber of our being. He wants wholehearted participants, not spectators.

God promises to meet with us. When we come into His presence, if our hearts and minds are truly engaged, He often overwhelms us with His goodness, His greatness, His Word. Think about the last time you truly "engaged" God—met with Him in a supernatural way. Has it been a while?

It's the Lord's desire that we come into His presence regularly, not in an "I have to get this over with" frame of mind, but a "Lord, I am so blessed to get to spend time with You!" attitude. When we meet with Him in that mind-set, the shining-greatness of the Lord will be revealed, and His glory will fill that place.

Lord, I long to meet with You—really meet with You. I don't want to
go through the motions, heavenly Father. I want Your glory to fall,
Your shining-greatness to overwhelm me. Today I offer myself to You,
not as a spectator, but a participant in Your holy presence. Amen.

REDEEMING LOVE

*"For a brief moment I forsook you, but with great compassion
I will gather you. In an outburst of anger I hid My face from you
for a moment, but with everlasting lovingkindness I will have
compassion on you," says the L*ORD *your Redeemer.*

Contrasting opposites are at work in this beautiful passage from Isaiah: a brief desertion but a great gathering; momentary anger but everlasting love and compassion. There is purpose in His every word. The Lord is passionate about His chosen people. Though they felt deserted, it was short-lived; God's intent was to gather them back with great care. He was angry and hid His face but could never deny His eternal love that would redeem them.

Just as God loved the Israelites and spoke to them through Isaiah, so does He love each of us. His heart has not changed through the ages. He still allows us times in which we feel deserted, yet He will pursue and draw us back to Himself. Sin still angers Him, but He is tender and merciful toward those He loves. His ultimate act of compassion for us was when He poured out His wrath on Jesus at the cross, when He gave His Son to be our Redeemer. He bought us back at the highest price when we had no way to bring ourselves to Him.

*Father, thank You for forgiveness and restoration.
In the dark times, help me to remember Your
everlasting love and grace toward me. Amen.*

GIVER OF GOOD THINGS

*For the L*ORD *God is a sun and shield: the L*ORD
will give grace and glory: no good thing will
he withhold from them that walk uprightly.

PSALM 84:11 KJV

Worry is such a useless practice, like spinning wheels on a vehicle that takes you nowhere. And yet we women are notorious for it. The Bible advises us to let each day take care of itself. We are promised that God will provide for us.

Psalm 84:11 says that God is not a withholder of good things from His children. He knows us. He created us and put into us our own unique dreams, preferences, and hopes. When you begin to worry, read this verse. Put it on your bulletin board at work and your bathroom mirror at home. Read it aloud each time worry begins to creep in.

Your heavenly Father is not "the big man upstairs" looking down upon you and laughing at the unfulfilled desires in your life. He wants to give you good things. Often His timing is different than ours, but His plan is always to bless and never to harm us. Look for the blessings in each day, and keep bringing your desires before the Lord in expectation.

Father, sometimes I wonder why You don't just pour
down from heaven the blessing that I cry out for.
Give me patience, and help me to see the good gifts
from You in each day—even the small ones. Amen.

....

....

....

....

....

....

OVERWHELMED BY LIFE

*"The waves of death swirled about me; the torrents
of destruction overwhelmed me. . . . In my distress
I called to the LORD. . . . From his temple he
heard my voice; my cry came to his ears."*

2 SAMUEL 22:5, 7 NIV

Some days the "dailyness" of life seems like a never-ending grind. We get up, eat, work, rest—and do it again the next day. Then when tragedy strikes, we're swept up in grief. What once seemed doable now seems a huge challenge. Depression sinks its claws deep into our spirit. Fatigue sets in, and we are overwhelmed: Life is hard. We may be tempted to question, "Is this all there is?"

Here's the good news: There's more. God never meant for us to simply exist. He created us for a specific purpose. He longs for us to make a difference and show others His love and grace. What's more, He never asked us to do life alone. When the waves of death swirl around us, and the pounding rain of destruction threatens to overwhelm us, we can cry out to our heavenly Father, knowing He will not let us drown. He will hear our voice, and He will send help.

So, next time you feel that you can't put one foot in front of the other, ask God to send you His strength and energy. He will help you live out your purpose in this chaotic world.

*Lord, thank You for strengthening me when
the "dailyness" of life, and its various trials,
threatens to overwhelm me. Amen.*

....

....

....

....

....

....

....

CONTENT IN HIM

But godliness with contentment is great gain.
1 TIMOTHY 6:6 KJV

Even the strongest Christian can struggle with discontentment. We're conditioned by the world to want more—of everything. More money, nicer clothes, a bigger house, a better-paying job. We're rarely satisfied with what we have.

When we're single, the "I Wish I Had This or That" list can get pretty long. If we don't get the things we long for—a spouse, children, a home, a better car, or nicer clothes, sometimes our discontentment shifts into overdrive. But what can we do about it?

Today, take stock of what God has already done for you. Take a look at the areas of your life in which you've been struggling with discontentment. Hasn't God already given you people who pour into your life? Hasn't He made sure you have a roof over your head and food to eat? Has He not provided you a way to get to and from work?

Instead of focusing on all of the things you don't have, spend some time praising Him for the things you do have. Offer the Lord any discontentment, and watch Him give you a contented heart.

Lord, I confess that I'm not always content. I find myself wishing life were different sometimes. Today I thank You for the many things You've already done in my life. Take my discontentment and replace it with genuine peace. Amen.

GRATITUDE

*Not that we are competent in ourselves to claim anything
for ourselves, but our competence comes from God.*

2 CORINTHIANS 3:5 NIV

In times of trouble or weakness, when circumstances seem beyond our control, we pray. But when life is moving along smoothly and we have a handle on life, it is easy to forget who God is and who we are.

Scripture teaches us that everything comes from God, even our achievements. Have you ever thought of your résumé as being God's work? When someone retires, do we thank God for their lifelong ability to work, to contribute, and to provide? Our good health, stable home, deep and abiding friendships. . .who gets credit for these?

Are you known for being prompt, polite, and professional? Who taught you those things? Who sent those teachers into your life?

Spend some time looking at the ordinary, good things in your life today—the things you take for granted as being yours. Pause to thank God for giving them to you. Acknowledge the Giver behind every good thing you have received or accomplished.

*Heavenly Father, I have been blind to the goodness that dwells in You.
I have moved through my days all too quickly and claimed as my own
doing the gifts You have bestowed. Thank You for all Your gifts to me. Amen.*

TAKE MY HAND

*I am not ashamed of it, for I know the one in whom I trust,
and I am sure that he is able to guard what I have
entrusted to him until the day of his return.*

2 TIMOTHY 1:12 NLT

Ever feel like giving up? Throwing in the towel? Some days it's hard to find the resolve to persevere. Despite our human frailties, our heavenly Father is there to grab our hands and pull us to our feet. He isn't impressed with what we do in life, but how we tackle each day. He wants us to gaze at Him and know He's there to take care of us despite the overwhelming odds life presents.

Paul could have given in. The man was shipwrecked, beaten, imprisoned, and persecuted, and yet he kept on giving the Lord praise. He preached the good news of Jesus and faced the consequences of his actions. Few of us will face the same persecution, but we have the same Spirit within us that Paul did. He told Timothy he had no regrets because he was sure of the One he served.

Are you sure today of the One you serve? When coming to grips with difficulties, do you turn to the Creator of the universe and ask for help? You should. He's available. Just reach out and take His hand. He'll be there.

*Lord, teach me Your love. Let me feel
Your embrace. I choose to trust in You. Amen.*

HOPE

*Why, my soul, are you downcast? Why so
disturbed within me? Put your hope in God,
for I will yet praise him, my Savior and my God.*

PSALM 42:5 NIV

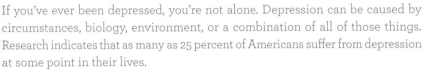

If you've ever been depressed, you're not alone. Depression can be caused by circumstances, biology, environment, or a combination of all of those things. Research indicates that as many as 25 percent of Americans suffer from depression at some point in their lives.

We are blessed with scriptural accounts of godly people like David and Jeremiah who struggled with depression. These stories let us know that it's a normal human reaction to feel overcome by the difficulties of life.

While feeling this way can be normal, it doesn't have to be the norm. As Christians, we have hope. Hope that our circumstances will not always be the way they are right now. Hope that no matter how dismal the world seems, God wins in the end. Hope that eternity is just on the other side.

Hope is like a little green shoot poking up through hard, cracked ground. When you're depressed, do what David and Jeremiah did—pour out your heart to God. Seek help from a trusted friend or godly counselor.

Look for hope. It's all around you, and it's yours for the taking.

*Father, even when I am depressed, You are
still God. Help me to find a ray of hope
in the midst of dark circumstances. Amen.*

A NEW SONG

He put a new song in my mouth,
a hymn of praise to our God.
PSALM 40:3 NIV

David was in a bad spot. He describes it in the Psalms as a "slimy pit. . .the mud and mire." Ever been there?

Often a person suffering from depression feels as if she is in a pit, unable to get out. Certainly a pit is not a place of rejoicing or singing!

Life is hard, and we are human. We make mistakes. We suffer. We fail. We lose. We crumble. Sometimes we can't even see God through the gray cloud of hopelessness.

Perhaps after losing a loved one or going through another difficult season in life, you felt as if you would never be happy again. Thankfully, one of the greatest gifts God gives His children is the gift of a "new song."

If you are in a place of sadness, trust in this. There will come a day, an hour, a moment when God will transform gloom into joy. Your feet will be planted on a mountain, where once you fought to climb out of a valley.

Be steadfast. Trust in the dark what He showed you in the light. Suffering is but for a time, and God's mercies are new every day.

Father, when You find me in the pit, put a new
song of praise in my heart, that I might live
again a life of abundance and joy. Amen.

IMMOVABLE LOVE

Every mountain and hill may disappear. But I
will always be kind and merciful to you; I won't
break my agreement to give your nation peace.
ISAIAH 54:10 CEV

Mountains are steadfast and immovable. Even small parts of mountains are not easily moved. Nature's forces take centuries or tremendous energy to do so. Snow, glacial ice, mountain streams, rain, and wind move one grain of sand or pebble at a time. Volcanoes release tremendous energy to alter a mountain's shape. When man wants to build a highway through a mountain range, the power of dynamite is needed to cut tunnels through rock, and the road must twist and turn to adapt to the terrain.

God says His love is even more immovable. Mountains will move before His love will leave us. Hills will depart easier than God would remove His covenant of peace with us. In the sacrifice of Christ on the cross, He demonstrated His amazing love for us, and Jesus became our peace. Romans 5:1 (ESV) says, "Therefore, since we have been justified by faith, we have peace with God through our Lord Jesus Christ." Regardless of what we have done or will do, God's love is set upon us. By faith, we have only to believe what Jesus has done for us.

Father, thank You for Your immovable love,
for the permanence of Your covenant of peace,
and for my righteousness, which does not come from
my good works but from Christ's sacrifice for me. Amen.

FIX YOUR EYES

So we fix our eyes not on what is seen, but on what is unseen,
since what is seen is temporary, but what is unseen is eternal.
2 CORINTHIANS 4:18 NIV

The majestic oak's enormous trunk was three feet in diameter. For more than one hundred years, buds had formed each spring and leaves had dropped each fall. But one spring, the leaves were not as plentiful as in previous years. That summer the leaves suddenly turned brown. Soon it was painfully obvious that the great white oak had died.

What a visual reminder that the things of this world will someday pass away. Although the oak had lived many years, it no longer produced oxygen—no longer shaded the backyard. Even trees have life spans.

There are very few things that can be counted on to last forever. Souls are eternal; they remain even when our earthly bodies decay. We need to see beyond the physical by focusing on the spiritual. There is life beyond what we are experiencing in this moment.

Spend your energy and resources on those things that will last: your relationships with your heavenly Father and with others. Love God. Love people. Then you won't fear being cut down like the majestic oak. You will live into eternity in the Lord's presence.

Dear Lord, help me keep an eternal focus and perspective
in this life. Allow me to "see" what is unseen. Amen.

....

....

....

....

....

....

....

RED HIGH HEELS

*Don't be concerned about the outward beauty of fancy
hairstyles, expensive jewelry, or beautiful clothes. You
should clothe yourselves instead with the beauty that
comes from within, the unfading beauty of a gentle
and quiet spirit, which is so precious to God.*

1 PETER 3:3-4 NLT

Fashion gurus love to tell women what to wear. Many like to recommend one
pair of red shoes—preferably sassy high heels—to spice up a lady's wardrobe.
Proponents of the advice say having one special pair of shoes to wear when
feeling down or depressed can turn a woman's whole day around, making her
feel beautiful and powerful.

While fashion trends are fun and we all want to look well-groomed, we can't
forget where true beauty and power come from. Wasn't it Jesus who taught us
not to place our treasure in physical things like our bodies or worry about where
our clothes will come from? He promises to provide for us.

Shoes scuff, necklaces break, and fabric fades, but true beauty starts from
within. When we allow God to dress our spirits in robes of love, joy, peace, patience,
kindness, goodness, faithfulness, gentleness, and self-control, our inner beauty
will far outshine anything we put on our physical bodies.

*Dear Father, I want to be a woman whose inner beauty far
surpasses my outer beauty, so that when people encounter me
they are pointed to You and rejoice in Your creation. Amen.*

REMEMBERING GOD'S MARVELOUS WORKS

Seek the Lord and His strength....
Remember his marvelous works that he hath done.
1 Chronicles 16:11–12 KJV

Jamie spent the last few months of a busy year taking care of her aging mother, commuting back and forth between her parents' home and her own. Her dad had died several months before, leaving Jamie's mom with a mountain of paperwork, financial stress, and unfinished business.

As an only child, Jamie felt the weight of responsibility. And she resented her dad for not leaving his affairs in better order. She even resented her mom for leaning on her only daughter too much.

Those were in the crazy moments. In her saner times, Jamie remembered that God had healed her dad of cancer not once, but twice, and he had enjoyed a long life of ministry and service. She recalled that her mom had found a Christian attorney who was helping them sort through her father's estate at a fraction of his normal fee. And she reminded herself that God had kept her safe on her weekly commute and given her extra money at just the time she needed it for gas and meals.

What marvelous works has God done in your life? How do you remind yourself of them? When times are hard, it's wonderful to look back in a journal or Bible and see His goodness, answers to prayers, and interventions recorded. It may keep you sane, and it will help you give thanks, even when the going is tough.

Lord, help me to remember that You have
done marvelous things for me. Amen.

FINANCIAL STRAIN

*"No one can serve two masters. Either you will hate the one
and love the other, or you will be devoted to the one and
despise the other. You cannot serve both God and money."*
MATTHEW 6:24 NIV

Do you ever get nervous when you watch the news and see reports about the stock market? Does your head spin when you see the prices rise at the gas pump? Can you feel your heart race when you look at your bills in comparison to your bank statement? Even though many of our day-to-day activities depend on money, it's important to remember that money does not provide or sustain. Only God can provide for you and sustain you. When we begin to focus on and worry about money, then we are telling God that we don't trust Him.

As you feel yourself start to worry about money, stop and change your focus from wealth to God. Thank Him for what He has provided for you and then humbly ask Him to give you wisdom about your financial situation. Be at peace as you remember that you can absolutely trust God to provide for you and to sustain you.

*Dear God, help me not to worry but to trust that You
will provide for me. Help me to be devoted to You only. Amen.*

HEAD AND SHOULDERS, KNEES AND TOES

*Even so the body is not made
up of one part but of many.*

1 CORINTHIANS 12:14 NIV

JoAnn struggled to fit in with the people in her neighborhood, and even the people in her church. She wondered if she would always feel like a square peg in a round hole. Convinced she would never find her place, she retreated to the safety of her home, where books and television became her primary source of comfort. In short, she gave up on trying to find her place in the body of Christ.

Perhaps you can relate to JoAnn. Maybe you're struggling to fit in. Remember, daughter of God, He has created you uniquely, with specific gifts. The body of Christ is made up of many members—all ages, colors, shapes, and sizes, with a variety of spiritual gifts.

Make a conscious decision today not to retreat. Even if you've struggled to fit in, give it another try. Pray about the specific gifts God has placed within you, then ask Him—and your church leaders—where you can best serve Him. You might be surprised at the new directions in which the Lord leads you.

*Father, I don't always know where I fit. Sometimes I feel there's
not a place for me, even at church. I know I'm a part of Your body,
and all the parts work together. So, stir up the gifts, Lord,
then place me where I can be most effective. Amen.*

REACH OUT

*But people who aren't spiritual can't receive these truths from God's
Spirit. It all sounds foolish to them and they can't understand it,
for only those who are spiritual can understand what the Spirit means.*

1 CORINTHIANS 2:14 NLT

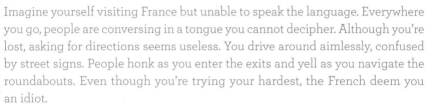

Imagine yourself visiting France but unable to speak the language. Everywhere you go, people are conversing in a tongue you cannot decipher. Although you're lost, asking for directions seems useless. You drive around aimlessly, confused by street signs. People honk as you enter the exits and yell as you navigate the roundabouts. Even though you're trying your hardest, the French deem you an idiot.

In the same way, unbelievers may feel confused trying to navigate the unfamiliar territory of spiritual truth. They don't have the ability to understand it because they don't have the Holy Spirit as a teacher to guide them. The Bible may not make sense to them, but don't be quick to judge. Hope isn't lost!

God likely has placed unbelievers in your life that He wants you to reach out to. Share your faith with them in words and actions they can understand. Pray the Lord opens their hearts to receive Jesus as Lord and Savior. Then the Holy Spirit will dwell with them, giving them the ability to comprehend spiritual truth. Pray that these lost "tourists" will find Jesus soon!

*Dear Lord, help me not judge those that
don't know You. Instead, may I pray that You
intercede to show them the way. Amen.*

PROTECTING ANGELS

*For he will command his angels concerning
you to guard you in all your ways.*
PSALM 91:11 NIV

The SUV was completely totaled after being rear-ended by a semitruck. After flipping end over end, the SUV landed upright. Mangled pieces from the vehicle were scattered along the highway.

It was hard to imagine anyone surviving in such an accident, but the five occupants—a husband and wife and their three granddaughters—walked away from the scene with minor injuries.

Have you ever experienced a miraculous accident like this? It wasn't luck that kept you safe; it was the protecting hands of God's angels watching over you just as the angels did for the family in the SUV.

Take great comfort in knowing that God loves you so much that you are guarded and protected by an elite group of heavenly host.

*Dear Lord, no matter where I go, in my heart
I always know that Your angels are with me night
and day, keeping me safe in every way. Amen.*

CONSISTENT RIGHTEOUSNESS, CONSTANT PEACE

How I wish that you had obeyed my commands!
Your success and good fortune would then
have overflowed like a flooding river.
ISAIAH 48:18 CEV

People are drawn to bodies of water. Pick any place on earth where there is a beautiful sea, lake, or river, and you'll find hotels, cabins, boats, marinas, docks—everything that goes with being near and enjoying the water. Many of us find we can relax easily near water. At the seashore, we are lulled by the rhythm of waves as they unceasingly roll in. At the river's edge, we are mesmerized by the current. The river is always moving downstream, an endless supply of water passing by.

Isaiah 48 tells us that if we follow God's commandments, our peace can be as constant as a river and our righteousness as consistent as waves at the shore. On the other hand, disobedience to God's commandments results in an inconsistent lifestyle and an interrupted peace. We should examine our lives in light of God's Word, asking the Holy Spirit to reveal areas where we do not follow His commandments. When we confess our sin, He is faithful to forgive us, and we can begin again. We can ask Him to help us believe that His way is right. We can ask for the desire and resolve to follow Him.

Lord, show me the areas in my life where I am not
paying attention to You. Lead me to consistent
righteousness and constant peace. Amen.

....

....

....

....

....

....

SLOWLY, STEADILY, SURELY. . .

"This vision is for a future time. It describes the end,
and it will be fulfilled. If it seems slow in coming, wait patiently,
for it will surely take place. It will not be delayed."

HABAKKUK 2:3 NLT

Ah, patience. It's the stuff frustration is made of. And yet it's a virtue the Lord expects His people to have plenty of.

In this fast-paced world, we want what we want and we want it *now*. We don't want to wait. And we don't wait—for most things. Microwaves speed up the cooking process. Fast-food restaurants hand us our food as we zip through the drive-thru. Internet access gives us instant access to people, places, and things all over the world. And cell phones give us the chance to connect with folks in a hurry.

Oh, if only we could learn the value of slowing down—of waiting in God's presence. Take another look at today's scripture. Sometimes the things we're waiting on come slowly. Similarly, God's plans may come slowly, but they come steadily, surely. God is going to do what He says He'll do. We don't know when, exactly, but we can be found faithful while we're waiting.

What are you waiting on today? Is your patience wearing thin? Apply the slowly, steadily, surely principle and watch God work—in His time.

Lord, I'm used to things moving fast.
And yet I find myself in a waiting season.
Give me patience, Lord, and remind me daily that
Your timetable is the only one that matters. Amen.

FORGIVE. . .AND FORGIVE AGAIN

Then Peter came to him and asked, "Lord, how often
should I forgive someone who sins against me?
Seven times?" "No, not seven times," Jesus replied,
"but seventy times seven!"
MATTHEW 18:21–22 NLT

Monica's grandmother had crossed the line once again. Every family gathering, without fail, Nana would start with the questions and hurtful remarks. Easter dinner was no exception: "Monica, why aren't you dating anyone yet?" "Don't you hear your biological clock ticking?" "Since you can't seem to find someone, I think you should sign up for a dating service."

People—even loved ones—sometimes say and do hurtful things that leave us feeling sad, bitter, or outraged. Maybe these people will realize they've wronged us and will ask for forgiveness, but often they—like Monica's grandmother—think they're helping and never know the hurt they cause us.

Instead of holding a grudge against these people, Jesus has another answer: Hand the hurt over to Him and forgive. Not just once or twice, but again and again. . .and again. Forgiveness is a process that is only successful with God's help. After all, He's the perfect example of forgiveness, forgiving us again and again. . .and again.

Jesus, You know the struggle I have in forgiving the
people who hurt me. Give me the strength I need to
completely let go of the bad feelings I have and
forgive them, just as You have forgiven me. Amen.

THINK ABOUT THIS

Whatever is true, whatever is noble, whatever is right, whatever is pure, whatever is lovely, whatever is admirable—if anything is excellent or praiseworthy—think about such things.
PHILIPPIANS 4:8 NIV

Jessica's friends jokingly called her obsessive, and deep down inside, Jessica knew they were right. But she couldn't help it. Once she started worrying about something, she just couldn't stop.

Lately she had been concerned about her brother, who was serving in the military overseas. She couldn't stop thinking about all that could happen to him, and it was starting to interfere with her life. She spent hours online every day, reading everything she could find about the country in which he was serving. After a few months she became withdrawn and depressed, not wanting to leave her house or her computer for even a few hours.

Our thought patterns can powerfully influence our emotions. This is no surprise to students of scripture—God's Word tells us to think about things that are positive, uplifting, praiseworthy, and true. And for good reason. When we dwell on dismal thoughts, we begin to believe them. When we believe them, we start to feel defeated and depressed. Positive thoughts have the opposite effect and can make a dramatic difference in our outlook on life. What negative thoughts do you need to eliminate today?

Lord, forgive me for the negative and self-defeating thoughts I've allowed to bring me down. Help me to think about things that honor You, and thank You for the way this changes my attitude and my heart. Amen.

SIMPLY SILLY

If you are cheerful, you feel good.
PROVERBS 17:22 CEV

Jeanne Calmont died at the age of 122, after outliving twenty-seven French presidents, and entered the *Guinness Book of World Records* as the world's oldest woman. When asked the secret of her longevity, she replied, "Laughter!"

It's a scientifically proven fact that laughter lowers blood pressure and strengthens the immune system. It helps overcome depression. In short, laughter is good medicine. A "spoonful" each day will add much to our lives.

Paul had so much joy that he sang and won his jailors to Christ. Imagine the effect we could have on our world today if our countenance reflected the joy of the Lord all of the time: at work, at home, at play. Jesus said, "I have told you this so that my joy may be in you and that your joy may be complete" (John 15:11 NIV).

Is your cup of joy full? Have you laughed today? Not a small smile, but laughter. Maybe it's time we looked for something to laugh about and tasted joy. Jesus suggested it.

Lord, help me find joy this day. Let me
laugh and give praises to the King. Amen.

YOU EITHER TRUST HIM
OR YOU DON'T!

*Trust in the LORD with all thine heart; and lean
not unto thine own understanding. In all thy ways
acknowledge him, and he shall direct thy paths.*

PROVERBS 3:5-6 KJV

"Trusting the Lord isn't always easy," Candace confided at her women's Bible study after they read Proverbs 3:5-6.

"You're right—it's not always easy, but it's pretty simple. You either trust Him or you don't," Sandy said.

Talk about an enlightening statement! It was straight to the point. True friends often tell you the truth just as they see it.

The world is filled with personal trials, and we often struggle with them alone. We may be worried about finances. The sudden loss of a family member or friend may grieve or depress us. A good friendship may be strained over misunderstanding or outright nastiness. No matter what the situation, trials often leave us feeling anxious and confused.

Today, if you're facing a difficult trial, try trusting the Lord with all of your heart. Not just a little piece of your heart, but all of it. Don't try to figure things out. God already has them under control and He holds all the answers to your unanswered questions.

Remember, it's really pretty simple, you either trust Him or you don't.

*Dear Lord, I trust You with all my heart and all
my being. I acknowledge You as Lord of my life.
Thanks for making it pretty simple. Amen.*

WHAT IS WRITTEN ON YOUR HEART?

These commandments that I give you today
are to be on your hearts. . . . Write them on the
doorframes of your houses and on your gates.
DEUTERONOMY 6:6, 9 NIV

In many Jewish homes today, there is a small container attached to the doorway. Inside the box is a tiny scroll containing the words of Deuteronomy 6:9. This is a *mezuzah* and serves as a tangible reminder of God's ancient covenant with the Israelites and His desire to have first place in their lives.

In the Old Testament, God's law was written on scrolls and passed down from generation to generation. In the New Testament, we learn that Jesus both fulfilled the old covenant and introduced a new covenant. This new covenant is written on our hearts (see Hebrews 10:16). God's Word is our scroll and it confirms the truths that He has already written on our hearts through the Holy Spirit. In spite of this, we sometimes forget.

What are some practical ways you can remind yourself, each day, of the truth of God's Word? Copy verses on index cards to carry with you, or better yet, commit them to memory. Listen to the Bible on CD or to songs composed from scripture. Whatever you do, always be looking for fresh ways to remember the truth that God has written on your heart.

Father, thank You for writing Your truth upon my heart.
Help me to look for tangible reminders of Your truth. Amen.

RUNNING ON EMPTY

I have observed something else under the sun.
The fastest runner doesn't always win the race, and
the strongest warrior doesn't always win the battle.
ECCLESIASTES 9:11 NLT

Jan struggled to be the best at everything she tried. She worked harder than anyone in her office, joined nearly every ministry at her church, taught wonderful Bible studies, and gave the best parties of anyone in her women's group. She cooked better, dressed better, kept a better home, and was never seen in public without her game face on.

There was only one problem. Before long, Jan was running on empty. She had little left to give. Her quest to appear perfect before a watching world crumbled around her. Not only was she not perfect, she couldn't keep up with her crazy schedule anymore.

Can you relate to this woman? Are you trying too hard? Always rushing here and there, involving yourself in a dozen things? Has keeping up appearances become an issue? Watch out. Before long, you might be running on empty too.

Lord, I'm so tired! I've taken on too much. My heart
was in the right place, but somewhere along the way
I got off-track. Redirect me, Father. Show me what
to give up and what to stick with. Amen.

A HOSPITABLE HEART

*Then after [Lydia] and her family were baptized, she kept
on begging us, "If you think I really do have faith in the Lord,
come stay in my home." Finally, we accepted her invitation.*
ACTS 16:15 CEV

Lydia, a dealer in purple cloth, worked hard at her trade. The Bible does not tell
us much else about her except that she was a worshipper of God.

One day during their travels, Paul and his companions stopped to pray by
the river outside the city gate of Philippi. They met a group of women there that
included Lydia. She listened to Paul's message and accepted Jesus. After Lydia
was baptized, she insisted the men come home with her and be her guests. As
was customary for a hostess, she likely prepared and served them food and gave
them a place to rest and pray. She showed hospitality in the name of the Lord.

You can follow Lydia's lead. Whether your home is small or large, you can
choose to be hospitable. Invite a friend who needs a pick-me-up to join you for a
meal during the week. Ask a single mom and her children to come over for a pizza
and movie night. If elderly neighbors are unable to get out, take your hospitality
to them! Bake them some cookies or take them flowers from your garden.

*Father, give me a heart for hospitality.
May I always serve others in Your name. Amen.*

CONTENTMENT

*A peaceful heart leads to a healthy body;
jealousy is like cancer in the bones.*
PROVERBS 14:30 NLT

Dawn was never happy. Just when she would get her apartment decorated the way she wanted it, a friend would purchase a new piece of furniture or paint a room, and suddenly Dawn wanted to have something similar. She would search online and in catalogs and stores for the perfect outfit, coat, or handbag and when she finally purchased it, she would second-guess her decision.

Dawn's problem was that she was never at peace. She was constantly comparing herself to other people and comparing her things to their things. In the comparison game, Dawn and her stuff never won. What other people had was always so much better.

Proverbs warns us against falling into this dangerous trap. When we compare ourselves to others we become jealous, and this jealousy has a way of growing like cancer—quickly and out of control. It can wreak havoc with our inner lives because we are never satisfied, never at peace.

The quickest way to avoid the comparison trap is to adopt an attitude of thankfulness, to focus on what we have rather than what we don't have, and to make peace with the idea that there is nothing in this world that can truly satisfy our souls. For true satisfaction, we must look to God and God alone.

*Heavenly Father, thank You for all You provide for me.
Guard my heart against comparing myself to others.
Help me to be at peace. Amen.*

I'VE GOT THE JOY, JOY, JOY, JOY...

You make known to me the path of life;
you will fill me with joy in your presence,
with eternal pleasures at your right hand.
PSALM 16:11 NIV

It's one thing to be single. It's another thing to be *happy* single. Maybe you read those words, cringe, and ask, "How can I ever be happy single?" Oh daughter of God, you can! In fact, your singleness puts you in the perfect spot for happiness because you've got time to pour into your relationship with your heavenly Father—the very giver of happiness.

Our Creator God is a joy-giver, and He pours it out when you need it most. At your very lowest point, He's there, ready to fill you with that bubbling-over kind of joy. And how wonderful to know that in His right hand there is happiness forever. Forever! That's a mighty long time. Longer than any earthly relationship, for sure!

Today, spend time with the Lord. Give Him your frustrations and fears. Ask Him to replace them with His overwhelming joy. Then begin to live out that joy in every other area of your life.

Oh Lord, I need Your bubbling-over joy today. Thank
You for the reminder that You are a joy-giver and
want me to be happy, not just in my singleness, but
in every aspect of life. Pour out Your joy, Father! Amen.

KNOWN BY GOD

But whoever loves God is known by God.

1 CORINTHIANS 8:3 NIV

How do we show that we love God? Is it by church attendance? Giving? Doing good deeds? Prayer? These may be manifestations of our love for God, or they may be things we do out of a sense of duty; but loving God is first and foremost a response to being known and loved by God. We can't muster emotion or feeling toward God nor do we love Him simply by willing ourselves to acts of obedience. We begin to love God when we grasp what it means to be known by God.

He knit us together in our mothers' wombs.

He knows the number of hairs on our heads.

He knows every quirk of our personality and gave us every talent that we have.

He accepts us as we are because of Christ's sacrifice for us.

He has compassion for our weakness.

He forgives our sins.

He longs to commune with us.

He delights to hear our prayers.

He desires to help us, strengthen us, and bless us.

He has given us the Holy Spirit as our Comforter, our Helper, and our Teacher.

He wills all this for us before we ever turn to Him in repentance. We need to reacquaint ourselves with the gospel often, to meditate on what Christ has done for us, and to remember that He first loved us.

*Lord, renew my love for You. Help me to
remember that You knew and loved
me before I ever knew You. Amen.*

NO WORRIES

*"So don't worry about tomorrow, for tomorrow will bring
its own worries. Today's trouble is enough for today."*
MATTHEW 6:34 NLT

What thoughts keep you up at night? Finances? Relationships? Work? Health or family concerns? We women are worriers by nature, but living in a constant state of dread isn't what God wants for us, His beloved daughters.

If we're honest with ourselves, we admit we sometimes hold on to our worries, thinking that keeping them close somehow keeps us in control of the situation. In reality, most of our worries concern things completely out of our hands.

Instead, Jesus offers us freedom from our chains of worry. "Trust Me instead of relying on yourself. Give Me the things that you fret over and stress about," He says. "How can you doubt that I'll take care of you when you mean so much to Me?"

Today, trust Jesus' assurance that He will take care of you. Ask Him to help you let go of your worrying nature and replace it with a spirit of praise and thanksgiving. It won't happen overnight, but soon you'll feel the true freedom from worry that only Jesus can supply.

Jesus, You know the toll my worries take on my heart and mind. I don't want to hold on to these negative thoughts, but it's hard to let go of them! Help me to place all my concerns in Your capable hands so that I can be free to praise You as You deserve! Amen.

....

....

....

....

....

....

....

THE ULTIMATE BEAUTY TIP

Charm is deceptive, and beauty is fleeting;
*but a woman who fears the L*ORD *is to be praised.*
PROVERBS 31:30 NIV

We live in a beauty-conscious world. Magazine covers, billboards, commercials, and TV shows try to tell us what we women need to look our best. The compulsion, "I've got to be beautiful," propels us to purchase makeup, clothes, shoes, and other "necessities."

There's nothing wrong with looking your best. In fact, it's a good thing. But if you've become obsessed with your appearance, then your priorities are out of balance. Remember, true beauty comes from the inside out. What's the point of going through the motions of having your hair and face done if you still have a sour expression? Besides, outward beauty is fleeting. Sooner or later the hands of the clock catch up with us.

Look to the Word of God for the definition of true beauty. It comes from the innermost places and is developed by spending time in the Word and in close relationship with the Lord. Even the plainest woman glows with the radiance of God when she's spent time with Him. There's no facial cream that even comes close.

Lord, I want to be seen as a beautiful woman—not just on the outside
but especially on the inside. Teach me Your beauty tips, Father.
Give me a heavenly radiance that only comes from above. Amen.

LEND A HAND

*"Which one of these three people was a real neighbor
to the man who was beaten up by robbers?"
The teacher answered, "The one who showed pity."
Jesus said, "Go and do the same!"*

LUKE 10:36–37 CEV

The woman pushed the button on her garage door opener and drove her car inside. Before she climbed out, she closed the garage door, intent on getting inside for her evening meal. She never noticed the bicycle lying in the grass or the boy who had tumbled onto the asphalt. Enveloped in the cocoon of her own home, she went about her business.

Too often, we follow a similar pattern. Our lives are busy—work, church, family, exercise, entertainment—and we never even meet our neighbors, much less get to know them.

While it's good to be cautious, the parable of the Good Samaritan tells us to help one another. Not only does becoming involved provide someone needed assistance, it expands our heart-reach. We become Jesus to others, spreading love and kindness, increasing our witness.

Let's keep our eyes peeled for occasions when we might help a neighbor. We want to be wise, select carefully, and love openly.

*Father, thank You for Your loving-kindness.
Give me an opportunity to share Your love with others. Amen.*

....

....

....

....

....

....

....

APPRECIATE WHAT YOU HAVE

"Thou shalt not covet thy neighbor's house,
thou shalt not covet thy neighbor's wife,
nor his manservant, nor his maidservant, nor his ox,
nor his ass, nor any thing that is thy neighbor's."
EXODUS 20:17 KJV

The dictionary defines the word *covet* as "having a strong desire to possess something that belongs to somebody else."

It is okay to want something. The danger comes when we want *what someone else has*. You probably don't struggle with coveting a neighbor's donkey, ox, or servant as the commandment suggests. But could it be a friend's husband that you wish were your own? A neighbor's swimming pool? A sibling's talent? A star's fame?

When God tells us that we "shall not," we must pay attention. His commandments are for our good. Catch yourself when you sense a desire for that which is not yours. Appreciate your own gifts, blessings, and belongings. An even higher calling is to be happy for others in their accomplishments and as they acquire possessions.

God, You have poured out so many blessings on me.
Protect my heart from desiring that which belongs to others. Amen.

LIGHT VS. DARKNESS

*But if we walk in the light as He is in the light,
we have fellowship with one another, and the blood
of Jesus Christ his Son cleanses us from all sin.*

1 JOHN 1:7 NKJV

Our world offers us endless choices. There are a multitude of dark paths to walk down, but only one that truly offers light. When we choose to walk with Jesus—the light of the world that casts away darkness—He will provide the illumination we need to make each day's choices.

At times you may be tempted to take a detour into darkness. It may not appear to make a big difference. Satan can convince you that doing something "just this once" will be of no real consequence. He tricked Adam and Eve that way in the Garden of Eden when he offered them fruit from the one tree God had declared forbidden.

Sometimes choices that the world offers you can be appealing. But anything that has the potential to hinder your walk with Christ is dangerous.

How do we remain in the light? We ask the Holy Spirit to guide us, and when we get an uneasy feeling regarding a choice, we pay attention to it. It may be hard to say no, but the payoff for obedience will be great.

Walk with others who walk with Christ. If you don't have Christian friends, take the initiative to attend a small-group Bible study, and you'll probably make friends as a side benefit. Christian friends can make all the difference in avoiding wrong paths.

*Father of Light, help me to be sensitive to Your
Holy Spirit. Shine Your light into my life. Amen.*

CALL ON GOD

*"Call to me and I will answer you and tell you
great and unsearchable things you do not know."*
JEREMIAH 33:3 NIV

Where do you go when you need answers? Friends, the internet, a parent, a boyfriend, or a minister?

All these resources can be great blessings to our lives. We all need Christian fellowship and godly counsel, particularly when we are puzzled or unsure about what to do. But the next time you are depressed or unsettled—when you find your mind racing with questions and the future seems far too big to face—call on God.

He is sovereign. He is before and after all things. He is Spirit. Yet He is accessible to each of His children at any time. He will not force His ways upon you. Our God gives us a lot of choice in this life, a lot of free will. But He does want to reveal His ways to us. He wants us to know His answers for our lives.

God may not give you all the answers you are seeking at once. He knows that some things you are not ready to know or to comprehend. Nonetheless, call on Him. Trust in Him. He will unfold the unknown to you as He sees best.

*God, teach me to call on You when I am tempted to
call on others instead. Thank You for being a Father
who longs to reveal Himself to me. Amen.*

KEEPING ON

Blessed is the one who perseveres.

JAMES 1:12 NIV

A child played with an inflatable superhero toy. When he punched the towering figure, it flopped over, then bounced back upright on its round base. Despite constant pummeling, nothing the child did could keep the superhero flat on its back.

We can feel like the superhero toy: We get knocked down by situations we cannot control. We're off balance, our breath thumped out of us. At these times, we need to adopt our own ability to bounce back.

The Book of James encourages us to persevere so we might attain "the crown of life that the Lord has promised to those who love him" (James 1:12 NIV). He reminds us that God is with us. When Satan attacks, finds our Achilles heel, and knocks us over, we need to dig deep into reservoirs of faith, tap into God's Word, and pop back up, fighting the fight He's put before us. We can't be passive, or we will be demolished.

Perseverance means staying in the fight and refusing to give up. This attitude empowers us and makes the victim mentality dissipate. It builds confidence, one fight at a time. Keep on keeping on—it's a powerful life tool.

Lord, give me the strength to get up from the mat and continue. I choose to believe in Your promises. Amen.

THE WELL-STOCKED PURSE

We can make our plans,
but the LORD determines our steps.
PROVERBS 16:9 NLT

Have you ever noticed how a woman will carry a purse, a diaper bag, a work satchel, a beach bag, and other totes appropriate for the occasion while men go empty-handed? She'll stuff everything from snacks to sewing kit to toilet paper in her bag. He'll shove his wallet in his pocket and is good to go.

Women want to be prepared for any and every crisis that may arise, while most men figure they will find, make, or otherwise produce whatever they need should an emergency cross their path. Women don't understand what seems to be neglect on the part of men, but that is just the way it is.

We women can plan every move we are going to make, but all the planning we do will not keep trouble away. We can horde all the things on our persons, in our cars, and in our houses that we think will make a problem manageable, but they cannot dam up the flood of emotions that come with a crisis.

Only God knows what tomorrow brings, and only He knows the tools we will need to get through any given situation. No packet of tissues or pocket-size scissors are going to be more useful than a spirit that is calm and trusts in the Lord.

Lord, help me to carry a peace-filled spirit with me at
all times, and I will trust You to guide me and to provide
for my needs along any path You may take me. Amen.

WHAT TO GIVE GOD

*Through Jesus, therefore, let us continually
offer to God a sacrifice of praise—the fruit
of lips that openly profess his name.*

HEBREWS 13:15 NIV

What can we possibly give God for what He has done for us through Christ? The only real gift we have to offer is praise.

Implicit in Hebrews 13:15 is a reminder of our identity as sinners in desperate need of the precious gift of righteousness through Jesus' sacrifice for us. Our own righteousness, consisting of our own human efforts, was filthy rags to God. Only Christ's righteousness could satisfy the divine justice of a holy God.

Jesus was willing to live among us, suffer, and die on the cross for us. He exchanged His life for ours. He took our filth and our punishment and gave us His righteousness and eternal life. God receives us based on this exchange.

How do we respond? With a sacrifice of prayer and praise. God desires to hear us praise Jesus, to speak of Him with gratitude, or to acknowledge our great need of Him. Pray in His name. Ask for the things Jesus promised. Pray Jesus' own words back to His Father in heaven. God is pleased with our faith in Jesus and our sacrifice of praise.

*Father, I praise You for clothing me in the righteousness of
Christ. May my life reflect His transformative grace. Amen.*

....
....
....
....
....
....
....

A "KEPT" HEART

Keep your heart with all diligence,
for out of it spring the issues of life.
PROVERBS 4:23 NKJV

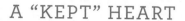

When you read the words "keep your heart," what comes to mind? Godly women keep many things: their purity, their word, and even their relationships. They are careful to guard these things from the evil one who seeks to steal them. Still, there is something far more important we should keep—something we often forget.

The Lord wants us to diligently guard and protect our hearts. Why? Because everything we are or ever will be comes from that very vulnerable place. In many ways, the heart is like a tiny spring that feeds a big river; out of it flow the issues of life. The heart is the hub, the center of our being. It's a place we often forget to protect, and the enemy knows it. He seeks to break our hearts or bring discouragement at every opportunity, particularly when we let our guard down.

Today, make a commitment to keep your heart with all diligence. Don't let past relationships, loneliness, or untapped dreams weaken you. Instead, stand strong against the enemy's attacks. And don't allow your heart to become tainted by the things of this world. Guard it. Protect it. Keep it.

Lord, I know You're interested in matters of the heart.
Who I am in my innermost being concerns You most.
Today I commit to "keep" my heart with all diligence.
Strengthen me from the inside out. Amen.

....

....

....

....

....

....

PRESENT HELP

*For I, the Lord your God, hold your right hand; it is
I who say to you, "Fear not, I am the one who helps you."*
ISAIAH 41:13 ESV

We shake hands to greet each other; it's a sign of welcome. We reach for the hand of a child when we're walking in a crowd or near a street; it helps protect and comfort the child. In times of great emotion or anticipation, we grab the hand of a nearby friend or family member; it says, "I am with you." By a hospital bed, we clasp the hand of a sick loved one; our hand tells them we are present, suffering with them. With every gripping of another's hand, we are bearing witness to God.

He holds your hand. He welcomes you into His kingdom. He protects you. He comforts you. He is with you in your most anxious moments and in your darkest hours. With the clasp of His hand comes courage for any situation. He tells you not to fear, for He is your ever-present help in times of trouble. He has a hold of you.

*Almighty God, I am grateful that You hold my hand. Forgive me
for the times I have forgotten this and let fear reign in my life.
Help me to remember I am never alone. Grant me the courage
that comes from knowing You as my helper. Amen.*

....

....

....

....

....

....

....

....

LET IT SHINE!

Let your light so shine before men, that they may see your
good works, and glorify your Father which is in heaven.
MATTHEW 5:16 KJV

Have you ever noticed the stadium lights at a sporting event? They not only illuminate the field, but they also put off a radiant glow that lights up the sky for miles.

The Bible says that Christians are the light of the world. As followers of Christ, we get to share the light of Jesus to those who may be living in darkness. How do we keep our lights shining bright? By staying connected to the true source of light, Jesus Christ, through prayer and Bible study.

Loving the unlovable, giving to the needy, forgiving the unforgivable, being honest, and striving to be Christlike are all perfect ways to share the light of Jesus. Let your life be a beacon of light and hope to all you meet. You are the light of the world, so let it shine and bring glory to Jesus Christ.

Dear Lord, thank You for bringing light to
my darkness. Help me to spread the light
of Jesus to those who don't know You. Amen.

WITH EVERY BREATH!

I will always praise the LORD.
PSALM 34:1 CEV

We humans are a self-centered bunch. Even those of us who have a personal relationship with the Creator often neglect to give Him the praise that He deserves. Instead, we choose to focus on our own problems and selfish desires. If we try to place praise high on our list of priorities, it's often difficult to follow through; praise isn't something that comes naturally to most of us.

So how can we develop a spirit of praise every day? First, amp up the amount of time you spend in prayer. As you go throughout your daily routine, find new reasons to offer thanks to the Father: the refreshment of a hot shower, a job to do, coworkers to interact with, food to satisfy hunger, the smile of a friend, the change of seasons. . .the list is endless!

Next, sprinkle your conversations with the hope your faith gives. Verbally acknowledge God's goodness and provision in your life and in the lives of others. Call a coincidence what it really is—the hand of the Father. Don't be afraid to let your newfound praise bubble over to every area of your life!

Father, You are my God, my almighty Redeemer and
Friend! I praise You because of the wonderful things
You do in my life every day. I praise You for being You!
Let everything within me praise the Lord! Amen.

WHAT ARE YOUR GIFTS?

There are different kinds of gifts, but the same Spirit distributes them.
There are different kinds of service, but the same Lord.
1 CORINTHIANS 12:4–5 NIV

A woman felt called by God to help out at her church, but she couldn't figure out which ministry best suited her. While some people were clearly Bible teachers, she was not. And while some could sing, she didn't feel that was her gifting. After spending time praying and seeking the Lord, she finally opted to work in children's ministry. She'd always done well with children, and she realized she could bless the little ones and fulfill her calling, all at the same time.

Maybe you know what it's like to search for your place. Perhaps you've tried different ministries and still haven't figured out your best place of service. Be patient. God has placed specific gifts within you, and you are needed in the body of Christ. Although your gifts may be different than someone else's, they are all from the same Spirit.

Today, thank the Lord for entrusting you with spiritual gifts. If you're struggling to know where you fit, ask Him to give you opportunities to minister in different areas until you find just the right spot.

Lord, thank You for pouring out Your Spirit on me,
and thank You for the gifts You've placed within me.
I want to reach others for You, so place me in
the very spot where I can be most effective. Amen.

GOD'S BLESSINGS

*The LORD bless thee, and keep thee: the LORD make
his face shine upon thee, and be gracious unto thee.*
NUMBERS 6:24–25 KJV

Once we have a relationship with God the Father through Jesus Christ, we are in line for a multitude of blessings. Billy Graham said, "Think of the blessings we so easily take for granted: life itself; preservation from danger; every bit of health we enjoy; every hour of liberty; the ability to see, to hear, to speak, to think—and to imagine all this comes from the hand of God." Without realizing it, we were blessed when we opened our eyes this morning. Some of us can add friends, family, freedom, and possessions to that list of blessings.

Why do we not recognize all of our blessings? Because it's human nature to zero in on what's wrong and miss what's right. We overcome that habit by praise and fellowship with Him. When we bless God in faithful praise and He blesses us, the result is a renewed strength for daily living.

God's love for us is eternal, as are His gifts. We need to open our arms and become thankful recipients for all He's given. Praise Him and bless His holy name.

*Lord, You have given me so much, and I am thankful.
Let me give thanks for Your gifts. Amen.*

COMFORT THE TROUBLED

*All praise to God, the Father of our Lord Jesus Christ. God is our
merciful Father and the source of all comfort. He comforts us in all
our troubles so that we can comfort others. When they are troubled,
we will be able to give them the same comfort God has given us.*

2 CORINTHIANS 1:3–4 NLT

Comfort is often associated with couches and cushions, leather seats of luxury
automobiles, and mattresses that adjust to fit the contours of our bodies. There
is comfort food like chicken potpie, potato soup, and mac and cheese. Some
clothing and shoe manufacturers promise comfort in their advertising.

If you have ever suffered a deep loss or an unbearable hurt in your life, then
you know the deeper meaning of the word *comfort*. You needed it, and hopefully
you received it.

God is the greatest source of comfort the human spirit will ever encounter.
God listens. He provides. At times, you can almost feel His hand stroking your
brow as He blesses you with sleep after many sleepless nights.

As God comforts us, we can comfort others. We particularly ought to reach out
to others who are facing a challenge we have faced ourselves. There is something
about the empathetic comfort of someone who has been in our situation that means
more than the sympathy of someone who hasn't.

Is there someone in your life who could use some comfort? Offer it in any
small way that you are able. The God of comfort has comforted you. So comfort
others in His name.

*Merciful Father, comfort me in my times of need
and show me those that I might comfort. Amen.*

....

....

....

....

....

TOSS THOSE BOXING GLOVES!

Avoiding a fight is a mark of honor;
only fools insist on quarreling.
PROVERBS 20:3 NLT

A woman struggled in her relationship with a particular friend. Though they'd known each other for years, they often found themselves disagreeing on things, sometimes even arguing. Whenever they got together, their quiet conversations evolved into heated discussions. Their personalities were vastly different, and they both tended to be a little stubborn. Neither wanted to give in, even though the things they argued about were sometimes silly. Would they ever just get along without all the quarreling?

Maybe you're in a complicated relationship with a friend. Perhaps she brings out the worst in you. She gets you stirred up. And yet, you love her. You don't want to see the friendship come to an end. What can be done to salvage it?

As with any relational issue, you approach it with a servant's heart. You've got to follow the golden rule—doing unto others as you would have them do unto you. And you've got to love others as you would love yourself. This is tough to do when you're arguing. But just how important is it to prove your point in the grand scheme of things? Important enough to sacrifice a friendship? Surely not.

Lord, I ask You today to be at the center of my
friendships, especially the difficult ones. Show me
what to say and what not to say to avoid strife.
Give me Your heart toward my friends. Amen.

ALL-EMBRACING WORSHIP

*I ask only one thing, L*ORD*: let me live in your*
house every day of my life to see how wonderful
you are and to pray in your temple.

PSALM 27:4 CEV

Sunday isn't the only day God wants us to spend time with Him. Sure, it's great to meet with other believers in corporate worship, but our worship shouldn't be limited to one place or time.

In addition to corporate worship, begin to seek God in your everyday life. Start by making a special quiet place in your house where you can spend time alone with God for Bible reading and devotions. While you are at work, open the window to enjoy God's creation or put an image of one of your favorite places on your computer's desktop. During your lunch break, work on memorizing a scripture and meditating upon it. When you get home in the evening, go to a local park and praise God for the plants and animals He has created. As you go to bed at night, turn on relaxing worship music so that you may praise Him as you drift off to sleep.

Ask God to help you find other ways to grow closer to Him. You will be blessed as you pursue a greater amount of quality time with God.

Dear Lord, let me be in Your presence all of my life.
Let me see Your beauty as I daily seek You. Amen.

THE WAITING GAME

Lord, I wait for you;
you will answer, Lord my God.

Psalm 38:15 NIV

Some researchers have estimated that Americans spend as much as two to three years of their lives waiting in line. We wait at the bank, the supermarket, the theater, and the airport. We wait for our paychecks, for Friday, and for vacation. It seems we are always waiting for something.

Waiting on God is just as hard. What are you waiting for today? Perhaps it's for financial deliverance, for a spouse, to finish school, or for your next big break. Perhaps you're waiting for the results of a medical test or news from your loved one in the military. Waiting can be downright agonizing. But God's Word tells us to wait patiently—with peace. Easier said than done, right? Rather than sighing with impatience, try praying, reading scripture, and making your waiting time productive and meaningful.

God's timing is certainly not ours. But as we wait on Him, we can be confident that He is never too early and never too late. Wait patiently and with confidence. God *will* come through.

Heavenly Father, when the waiting seems unbearable,
remind me that Your timing is always perfect. Amen.

GOD HAS LEFT THE BUILDING

And the curtain of the
temple was torn in two.
LUKE 23:45 NIV

On the day of Christ's death on the cross, all of creation was affected as the earth shook and the skies turned black. Inside the Jerusalem temple, the thick curtain separating the people from the inner room was split in two by a power unknown to man.

God, who had dwelled in the temple, the holy of holies, and had talked to Zechariah there (Luke 1), left the building when the curtain ripped on crucifixion day. He left a man-made structure to go and make a new home inside each individual who would invite Him in.

No longer did people have to physically move to Him to offer sacrifices and pray. Now God came to each individual on a personal level that was never known before. He made Himself accessible to anyone in any country on any continent.

God is an unchanging God who seeks relationship with us just as He did throughout biblical history. But we no longer have to walk the streets of Jerusalem to find God's Spirit. He comes and finds us just where we are.

Holy God, I invite You to make Your temple within me. I pledge
that all I do will show honor to You and give You praise. Amen.

A HOPE AND A FUTURE

"For I know the plans I have for you," declares the LORD, *"plans to prosper you and not to harm you, plans to give you hope and a future. Then you will call on me and come and pray to me, and I will listen to you. You will seek me and find me when you seek me with all your heart."*

Deb struggled with financial issues. She fought to keep her head above water. When the rent came due, or an unexpected bill arose, she scraped the bottom of the financial barrel to cover the costs. There were instances when she went without medical care. And socializing with friends? Out of the question. At times, Deb wondered what sort of future she might have. Would the stresses ever end?

Perhaps you can relate to Deb's story. Maybe you've gone through seasons of financial lack. Perhaps you're in one now. How wonderful to realize that God promises to give you not just hope, but a future. He longs for you to call out to Him, even from your need, your lack. Begin to see your future as He sees it, full of hope.

Today, give your future to God. He already owns it, anyway. Release it. Stop worrying about it. Don't fret over it. And remember to seek after the Lord with all your heart, even when times are tough.

Lord, sometimes financial issues scare me. They can be overwhelming. In those moments, I lose heart. Remind me, Father, that You've got plans for my hope, my future. Amen.

WELL OF SALVATION

With joy you will draw water
from the wells of salvation.
ISAIAH 12:3 NIV

In biblical times, wells were of great importance. Digging a well meant you planned to stay in one place. Owning a well meant your family possessed the surrounding countryside. Wells were gathering places and landmarks. People went to the well daily to get water for drinking, cooking, and cleaning. A well was essential to life for man and beast.

Our salvation is also a well. In it is not only our eternal life, but also our abundant life while we live on earth. Christ is the living water, continually refreshing and nourishing us, giving life to our bodies and souls. He is strength when we are weak, wisdom when we are foolish, hope when we are despondent, and life when we are dying.

Just as a bucket is lowered into a deep well, what begins as a descent into unknown darkness and depth becomes the means by which we draw up the water of life. Colossians 2:12 (CEV) says, "When you were baptized, it was the same as being buried with Christ. Then you were raised to life because you had faith in the power of God, who raised Christ from death." We have died with Christ and now we live, but daily we need to go the well of our salvation, remembering our need for Jesus' life, and drawing out the living water with joy.

Lord, thank You for saving me. Thank You for being
the living water, my continual source of peace,
comfort, strength, and joy. Cause me to remember
that my life is hidden in Yours. Amen.

LETTING GO

*As God's chosen people, holy and dearly loved, clothe yourselves with
compassion, kindness, humility, gentleness and patience. Bear with
each other and forgive one another if any of you has a grievance
against somone. Forgive as the Lord forgave you.*

COLOSSIANS 3:12–13 NIV

Christine knew she needed to forgive her friend Susie. She valued the relationship
and wanted to make things right. But she couldn't stop rehearsing her grievance
in her mind. How could Susie have been so thoughtless? The harder Christine
tried to make herself forgive, the further away forgiveness seemed.

A short time later, Christine was preparing a meal for Susie after her father
died. She began praying for Susie, and her heart broke in grief—she knew how
it felt to lose a parent. The feelings of injustice that seemed so deep-rooted were
replaced by feelings of kindness and compassion. By the time Christine delivered
the meal, she realized she'd forgiven Susie.

We talk about "working toward forgiveness," but this effort can be
counterproductive. Instead, Jesus wants us to show His compassion for others,
to think of ways to treat them with kindness and patience, and to pray that
God would help us to see the person through His eyes. As we do these things,
patiently and consistently, one day we will wake up and realize that forgiveness
has replaced our pain.

*God, I cannot express how grateful I am that You
have forgiven me for the many things I've done to hurt
You. Please help me to see the person who's wronged
me through Your eyes and to bestow on them the
same gift You've given me. Amen.*

DAUGHTER OF THE KING

So in Christ Jesus you
are all children of God.
GALATIANS 3:26 NIV

Galatians 3:26–29 are packed with statements about who you are as a Christian. You are Abraham's seed. You are an heir according to God's promise. And best of all, you are a *child of God*. Galatians reminds us that there is no male or female, race, or social status in the Lord's eyes. Believers are truly *one in Christ*.

You may have had a wonderful upbringing with loving parents. Or you may not have been as fortunate. You may have spent years in the foster system or had abusive parents.

Whether your childhood reflected love or abandonment, there is good news! As a Christian, you are a daughter of the King of Kings, the Lord of Lords, the sovereign God. He is the One who hung the stars in the sky, and yet He knows the number of hairs on your head. You are not just God's friend or distant relative. You are His *daughter*!

If you have a child of your own, consider the unconditional love you feel for him or her. As intense as that love is, because you are human, you are limited in your ability to love. In contrast, God loves us in a way we will not fully understand until we reach heaven. He is our *Abba Father*, our "Daddy."

Thank You, Father, for adopting me through
Christ as Your daughter. Teach me to live
as a reflection of Your love. Amen.

KEEP RUNNING

*Let us run with perseverance
the race marked out for us.*
HEBREWS 12:1 NIV

Karen began the marathon filled with confidence. She had been training for months. She knew the course well and trusted her body. The weather was perfect. But ninety minutes later, she was overcome with a fatigue like none she had ever known. Not only was she exhausted, she was nauseated. Her feet and legs screamed for mercy. She paused at a water station and considered giving up completely. She was about to step off the course and call it a day when a seasoned runner approached her. "Looks like you're having a hard time," she said cheerfully. Karen mustered a weak smile.

"Come on—I'll run with you for a while. See that sign up ahead? Think you can make it at least that far?" Karen willed her body to continue. For the next few miles, her companion slowed her own race to keep pace with Karen's. Every half mile or so she pointed out a goal to reach—mailboxes, stoplights, street signs. Thirty minutes later, Karen felt her strength return, buoyed by her new friend who clearly knew the value of a traveling companion. Finally Karen made it to the finish line. She was exhausted and overwhelmed, but grateful—grateful she had endured and grateful for a friend who helped her along the way.

*Father, when the race is too much for me, give me strength
for the journey. Thank You for the friends I have along
the way. Help me to finish with confidence. Amen.*

LAYING DOWN YOUR LIFE

This is how we know what love is:
Jesus Christ laid down his life for us. And we
ought to lay down our lives for our brothers and sisters.

1 JOHN 3:16 NIV

Jesus displayed the ultimate love for us when He gave His life on Calvary to pay for our sins. He laid down His life. And He asks us to do the same. But what does that mean? Can we really lay down our lives for others? If so, what does that look like?

We lay down our lives for others when we put their needs before our own. This can happen in a number of ways. First, we need to get past any selfishness in our lives and begin to adopt the "others first" attitude Jesus taught. That means we won't always get our way. It also means we have to have a servant's heart—even when it's difficult.

Today, take a close look at the people God has placed in your life. Is there someone you should be laying down your life for? What can you do to place this person's wants and needs above your own? Ask the Lord to help you implement His "others first" mentality. No, it won't be easy; yes, it will be worth it.

Lord, it's not easy to have a servant's heart. But You expect
no less from me. This is how we know what love is, Father.
You showed us by example. Today, please show
me whom I can lay my life down for. Amen.

READY FOR BATTLE

*So put on all the armor that God gives. Then when
that evil day comes, you will be able to defend yourself.
And when the battle is over, you will still be standing firm.*
EPHESIANS 6:13 CEV

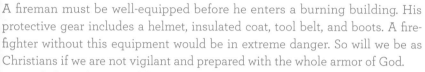

A fireman must be well-equipped before he enters a burning building. His protective gear includes a helmet, insulated coat, tool belt, and boots. A fire-fighter without this equipment would be in extreme danger. So will we be as Christians if we are not vigilant and prepared with the whole armor of God.

Evil abounds in our fallen world, and there are temptations around every corner. The devil never takes a day off. Be wary. We need to turn away from the lure of evil and place our lives in the center of God's will. In Ephesians 6, Paul lists the armor needed to battle the enemy: a breastplate of righteousness, boots of peace, the shield of faith, the helmet of salvation, and the sword of the Spirit.

Yield to God in prayer and call on His powerful presence. He'll be right beside you, ready for battle.

*Lord, help me to keep my armor and obey Your
Word so the ultimate victory will be Yours. Amen.*

CORE STRENGTH

He gives strength to the weary
and increases the power of the weak.
ISAIAH 40:29 NIV

A regular exercise program is essential to keep our bodies functioning the way God designed them to. One of the components of an effective exercise regime is the development of core strength. These muscles—the abdomen, trunk, and back—are responsible for strength, stabilization, and balance. Strong core muscles protect our spines, enable us to stand and move gracefully, and prevent the development of chronic pain. Investing the time and energy in developing and maintaining core muscles pays enormous dividends.

The same is true for our spiritual core muscles. Our spiritual core consists of foundational elements from which our lives move. It can include core beliefs—about who God is and the role of the Father, Son, and Holy Spirit in our daily lives.

Another spiritual core muscle can be principles on which we build our lives—what is our purpose on earth? What is our motivation for working, living, and interacting with others? Who are we in Christ? We can exercise our spiritual core by reading God's Word every day, praying about everything, and spending time in fellowship with other believers.

A strong spiritual core will help ensure that you remain stable and secure in a changing world. That you are able to keep from falling and that you are able to move and live gracefully. As you exercise your physical body, also make a commitment to regularly exercise your spiritual core as well.

Father, help me to return again and again to the
core foundations of my spiritual health. Amen.

THE WHITE KNIGHT

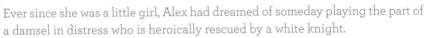

*Then I will rejoice in the L*ORD*.*
I will be glad because he rescues me.
PSALM 35:9 NLT

Ever since she was a little girl, Alex had dreamed of someday playing the part of a damsel in distress who is heroically rescued by a white knight.

Reality soon set in.

"How long am I supposed to wait for him?" she lamented to a friend over lattes. "My white knight apparently has a problem with punctuality."

We're all waiting for someone to rescue us. Maybe you're waiting for a soul mate to fill a void in your heart. Or perhaps you're waiting for a friend to come through in your time of need. It could be that you're waiting for your mom to finally treat you like an adult or for a prospective employer to call back with a job offer. We wait and wait and wait for a rescuer to come.

The truth is, God doesn't want you to exist in a perpetual state of waiting. Live your life—your whole life—by seeking daily joy in the Savior of your soul, Jesus Christ. And here's the best news of all: He's already done the rescuing by dying on the cross for our sins! He's the *true* white knight who secured your eternity in heaven.

Stop waiting; seek His face today!

Jesus, I praise You because You are the rescuer of my soul. Remind me of this fact when I'm looking for relief in other people and places. You take care of my present and eternal needs, and for that I am grateful. Amen.

....

....

....

....

....

....

....

A COMFORTABLE PLACE

*Don't you realize that your body is the temple
of the Holy Spirit, who lives in you and was given
to you by God? You do not belong to yourself.*

1 CORINTHIANS 6:19 NLT

Sandra spent the day picking up her apartment. She purchased a new bedspread for her guest room. On the coffee table, she placed a vase of fresh wildflowers. She got a magazine and set herself to work finding some new recipes for dinner.

Why did she take the time to do all these things?

Sandra's friend from out of state was coming to stay the weekend. She knew that her home was a reflection of herself. The effort that she took in preparing it for her guest would show that she cared enough to make her friend feel at home.

We take the time to make our homes comfortable and beautiful when we know visitors are coming. In the same way, we ought to prepare our hearts for the Holy Spirit who lives inside of us. We should daily ask God to help us clean up the junk in our hearts. We should take special care to tune up our bodies through exercise, eating healthful foods, and dressing attractively and modestly.

Our bodies belong to God. They are a reflection to others of Him. Taking care of ourselves shows others that we honor God enough to respect and use wisely what He has given us.

*Dear Lord, thank You for letting me belong to You.
May my body be a comfortable place for You. Amen.*

MAGNIFYING LIFE

With all my heart, I will praise the Lord.
Let all who are helpless, listen and be glad.
Honor the Lord with me! Celebrate his great name.

PSALM 34:2–3 CEV

To magnify is to make larger, more visible, more easily seen. When the angel of the Lord appeared to Mary telling her she would be the mother of the Messiah, her response was to quote the Psalm (ESV), "Oh, magnify the Lord with me." Mary knew she was the object of God's favor and mercy. That knowledge produced humility. It is the humble soul that desires that God be glorified instead of self.

Try as we might, we can't produce this humility in ourselves. It is our natural tendency to be self-promoters, to manage the impressions others have of us, and to better our own reputations. We need the help of the Spirit to remind us that God has favored each of us with His presence. He did not have to come to us in Christ, but He did. He has chosen to set His love on us. His life redeemed ours, and He sanctifies us. We are recipients of the action of His grace.

Does your soul make its boast in the Lord? Does your life make Christ larger and easier for others to see? Maybe you can't honestly say you desire this. Start there. Confess that. Ask Him to remind you of His favor and to work humility into your life, to help you pray like Mary did.

Christ Jesus, help me to remember what You have done
for me and desire for others to see and know You. Amen.

SPIRIT OF POWER

*So shall they fear the name of the LORD from the west,
and his glory from the rising of the sun. When the
enemy shall come in like a flood, the Spirit of the
LORD will lift up a standard against him.*
ISAIAH 59:19 KJV

Hurricane season comes every summer, and many of us watch weather reports and marvel at the damage wind can do. Strong winds stir the water and move it inland causing storm surges, rainstorms, and flooding. The power is in the wind, picking up water and moving it for miles.

God's Spirit is like wind having its way in a hurricane. His Spirit is more powerful than anything that comes into our lives. Health concerns, finances, and an uncertain future can threaten our peace of mind. Floods can come as anger, fear, depression, or despair. Uncontrolled emotions, addictive behaviors, anxiety, and loneliness can overwhelm us. In times like these, knowing the power of the name and glory of the Lord is essential. His name is above every other name; none has more authority than the One who spoke the world into being. His glory fills the whole earth.

When we cry out to God in the storms of our lives, we are calling on the most powerful force of all—the One who has the power over death.

*Lord, forgive me for forgetting how powerful You
are and that Your glory is displayed throughout the
whole earth. Help me remember whom my God is. Amen.*

....

....

....

....

....

....

UNDERSTAND. . .THEN ACT

*Make the most of every opportunity in
these evil days. Don't act thoughtlessly,
but understand what the Lord wants you to do.*
EPHESIANS 5:16–17 NLT

An elderly woman found herself acting on impulse—a lot. When things would go wrong, she'd react, and not always in a good way. She would blurt out things she didn't really mean. Sometimes she even made issues out of nothing. Then later—in the quiet times—she would wonder why. If she'd just taken the time to think before speaking, so many problems could have been avoided.

Can you relate to this woman? Do you ever act or speak without thinking first? If so, you are certainly not alone. Women are emotional and often knee-jerk, based on emotions. We're especially vulnerable when our feelings are hurt. We don't always take the time to understand what the Lord wants us to do before implementing our own plan of action.

Are you an actor or a reactor? Are you a thinker or a knee-jerker? The Lord longs for us to think before we act or speak—to act on His behalf. To react takes little or no thought, but to live a life that reflects the image of Christ takes lots of work!

*Lord, I don't want to be a reactor. I want to be an
actor—reflecting You in my life. Today, I give You my
knee-jerking tendencies. Guard my words and actions,
Father. Help me to think before I speak. Amen.*

PUT ON A HAPPY FACE

*He restoreth my soul: he leadeth me in the
paths of righteousness for his name's sake.*

PSALM 23:3 KJV

Sometimes we become discouraged with the direction of our lives. Circumstances are not of our choosing, not the plan we laid out. God's timetable isn't meshing with ours. But to keep others around us pacified, we paste on a smile and trudge through the murky waters.

Be encouraged. The Lord has promised He hears our pleas and knows our situations. He will never leave us. Our God is not a God of negativity, but of possibility. He will guide us through our difficulties and beyond them. In *Streams in the Desert*, Mrs. Charles E. Cowman states, "Every misfortune, every failure, every loss may be transformed. God has the power to transform all misfortunes into 'God-sends.'"

Today we should turn our thoughts and prayers toward Him. Focus on a hymn or praise song and play it in your mind. Praise chases away the doldrums and tips our lips up in a smile. With a renewed spirit of optimism and hope, we can thank the Giver of all things good. Thankfulness to the Father can turn our plastic smiles into real ones, and as the Psalm states, our souls will be restored.

*Father, I'm down in the dumps today.
You are my unending source of strength.
Gather me in Your arms for always. Amen.*

LOVE, NOT DUTY

I will take away their stony, stubborn heart and give
them a tender, responsive heart, so they will obey
my decrees and regulations. Then they will truly
be my people, and I will be their God.
EZEKIEL 11:19–20 NLT

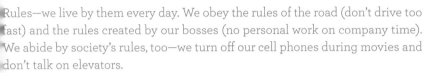

Rules—we live by them every day. We obey the rules of the road (don't drive too fast) and the rules created by our bosses (no personal work on company time). We abide by society's rules, too—we turn off our cell phones during movies and don't talk on elevators.

As believers, we try to obey God's rules. We attempt to do God proud by not taking His name in vain and by going to church and giving money to ministries. We speak of Him when the opportunity arises, listen to godly music, and even wear Christian T-shirts!

But how much of our obedience is out of a sense of duty? After all, God wants us to obey Him *not* because we're afraid He'll punish us if we don't, but because we love Him.

If you obey out of a sense of obligation, ask God to change your heart. Consider all He's done for you—given you His Son, forgiven your sins, answered your prayers. Remind yourself that He gave of Himself freely, with no strings attached.

When You meditate on His character and are convinced of His love for you, obedience will become not a duty but a delight.

Father, I praise You for the love that left heaven
behind. Help me to love You more. Amen.

STAND STRONG!

A final word: Be strong in the
Lord and in his mighty power.
Ephesians 6:10 NLT

Have you ever thought about how strong God is? With the strength of His Word, He spoke the planets and stars into existence. That same strength pushed back the Red Sea so the Israelites could cross over. It was His strength that gave David the courage to face Goliath. It was His strength that helped Joshua face his enemies at Jericho. His strength invigorated Naomi and Ruth, and it resides inside every believer who calls on the name of Jesus.

How wonderful to realize we have such power at work within us. The very God of the universe strengthens us with His might, not ours. If it were up to us, we'd make a mess of things, wouldn't we? Oh, we might muster up a little strength on good days, but what about the bad ones?

Perhaps you've never fully understood what it means to tap into God's strength. Maybe you still don't feel strong. Begin to memorize scriptures like the one above. Put notes on your mirror, your refrigerator, and your bedside table as a reminder. Then begin to quote those scriptures on a daily basis and watch His strength within you begin to grow!

Lord, in myself I'm weak. I'm totally dependent on You.
Thank You that the same strength that resided in
David, Joshua, Naomi, and Ruth lives in me.
In Your mighty power, I am strong! Amen.

ONE STEP AT A TIME

With your help I can advance against a troop;
with my God I can scale a wall.

PSALM 18:29 NIV

Sandi returned home from the doctor feeling discouraged and defeated. She knew she had put on a few pounds since her last visit, but was shocked when she saw the number on the scale. Her shock turned to humiliation when the doctor frankly addressed it. "Sandi, your health is on the line. If you don't lose at least seventy-five pounds, the next time I see you you'll be in a hospital bed. Your heart simply cannot take the strain of the excess weight you're carrying."

Seventy-five pounds! It seemed like an insurmountable goal. But a year later, when Sandi returned to the doctor for her annual check-up, she beamed when he looked at her chart. "Congratulations on your weight loss," he said. "How did you do it?"

Sandi smiled, "One pound at a time."

We often become discouraged when we face a mountain-size task. Whether it's weight loss or a graduate degree or our income taxes, some things seem impossible. And they often *can't* be done—not all at once. Tasks like these are best faced one step at a time. One pound at a time. Chipping away instead of moving the whole mountain at once. With patience, perseverance, and God's help, your goals may be more attainable than you think.

Dear Father, the task before me seems impossible.
However, I know I can do it with Your help. I pray
that I will trust You every step of the way. Amen.

SILENCE

He was oppressed and afflicted, yet he did not open his mouth;
he was led like a lamb to the slaughter, and as a sheep before
its shearers is silent, so he did not open his mouth.

ISAIAH 53:7 NIV

Jesus fulfilled Isaiah's prophecy by remaining silent before His accusers prior to His crucifixion. This fact is surprising to read because it goes against everything in us as humans—we can't imagine being falsely accused and not seeking to vindicate ourselves.

Jesus' silence can teach us important lessons. Underneath His silence was an implicit trust in His Father and His purposes. Christ knew whom He was and what He had come to do.

Perhaps He was praying silently as He stood before Pilate. It is often in the stillness of our lives that we hear God best. When we take time to think, meditate on scripture, pray, and reflect, we find we can indeed hear the still, small voice. Many of us avoid quiet and solitude with constant noise and busyness. But important things happen in the silence. The Father can speak; we can listen. We can speak, knowing He is listening. Trust is built in silence, and confidence strengthens in silence.

Lord Jesus, help me to learn from Your silence.
Help me to trust You more so I don't feel the need
to explain myself. Give me the desire and courage
to be alone with You and learn to hear Your voice. Amen.

DELIGHTFUL STUDY

Great are the works of the LORD;
they are pondered by all who delight in them.

PSALM 111:2 NIV

An accomplished pianist and a skilled tennis player both know that the more they practice, the more enjoyment they get out of their skill. Someone who has studied furniture design can value a fine antique that another person sees as a plain brown chest. A chef can taste and enjoy flavors the average palate cannot identify.

Have you ever thanked God for the pleasure of an orderly column of numbers in a balanced ledger? Ever noticed the shelves at the pharmacy and thanked God for all the research and discovery that led to such life-saving medications? Have you picked produce from your own garden and praised God for the delight of harvesting?

Your delight in God's creation is a gift from Him and an offering of praise back to Him for what He has done. To be thankful for the interest God gives you in creation brings glory to Him and leads to knowing and appreciating Him more.

Great God of all creation, Giver of all good things,
thank You for the endless beauty and wisdom in
the world around me that speaks of You. Amen.

....

....

....

....

....

....

....

....

....

REJOICING WITH FRIENDS

*"Then he calls his friends and neighbors together and says,
'Rejoice with me; I have found my lost sheep.' "*
LUKE 15:6 NIV

Gathering with friends and family can be so much fun, especially when you have something to celebrate. Birthday parties, weddings, and anniversaries are a blast when you're celebrating with people you love. There's something about being together that adds to the excitement.

God loves a good party, especially one that celebrates family togetherness. Just like the good shepherd in today's verse, He throws a pretty awesome party in heaven whenever a lost child returns to the fold. Celebrating comes naturally to Him, and—since you're created in His image—to you, too!

Think of all the reasons you have to celebrate. Are you in good health? Have you overcome a tough obstacle? Are you handling your finances without much grief? Doing well at your job? Bonding with friends or family? If so, then throw yourself a party and invite a friend. Better yet, call your friends and neighbors together, as the scripture indicates. Share your praises with people who will truly appreciate all that the Lord is doing in your life. Let the party begin!

*Lord, thank You that I'm created in the image of a God
who knows how to celebrate. I have so many reasons to
rejoice today. Thank You for Your many blessings.
And today I especially want to thank You for giving
me friends to share my joys and sorrows. Amen.*

DESPERATE FAITH

*And he said unto her, Daughter, thy faith hath made
thee whole; go in peace, and be whole of thy plague.*

MARK 5:34 KJV

When Jesus healed the woman with the hemorrhage, He commended her faith.
She had exhausted all her resources on doctors to no avail. Without addressing
Jesus at all, she simply got near Him in a crowd and touched His clothes. Instantly
His power healed her, and He knew that she had reached out to Him in a way
no one else in the pressing throng had. What was unusual about this woman's
touch? Why would Jesus commend her faith?

Maybe in her touch He felt her complete emptiness and need. She had
nowhere else to turn. He was the source of healing power. Her faith was an act
of utter dependence; it was Jesus or nothing.

Proverbs 3:5–6 tell us to trust in the Lord with all our hearts and not lean on
our understanding. This is hard to do, since we prefer to trust in the Lord along
with our own understanding of how things should work out. Though we are given
minds to read, think, and reason, ultimately our faith comes from abandoning
hope in ourselves and risking all on Jesus.

*Lord, I am often blind to my own weakness and my need of You.
Help me trust You the way this sick woman did. Amen.*

FEAR VS. TRUST

Fear of man will prove to be a snare,
but whoever trusts in the LORD is kept safe.
PROVERBS 29:25 NIV

We all experience fear. It creeps up on us like a shadow in a dark alley when we are least expecting it. A relationship ends. Suddenly, you fear. You lose your job. Fear raises its ugly head again. Someone close to you dies. Fear. Your bills pile up. Fear. Perhaps it is a diagnosis, an entangling sin that seems unconquerable, or even a person that you fear.

Fear has an enemy called Trust. When Fear senses Trust trying to break into any situation, it puts on boxing gloves and prepares for a fight. You see, Fear is from Satan, and the father of lies does not give up his attacks on you easily. Trust is an archrival. Fear knows it will take all it's got to beat Trust and remain standing strong when the bell rings.

When you are afraid, speak the name of Jesus. Speak it over whatever problem or uncertainty is on your mind. Speak it over medical results, financial worries, and even unreasonable fears such as phobias or paranoia.

Fear is a snare, but trusting in the Lord brings safety. Fear is not as tough as it thinks it is. It will be knocked out of the ring when you tackle it with Trust.

Lord Jesus, help me to trust in You more each day. When I feel
afraid, remind me to speak Your name over my worry. Amen.

WHAT DO YOU KNOW?

*Hold on to instruction, do not let it go;
guard it well, for it is your life.*
PROVERBS 4:13 NIV

We learn valuable lessons from every experience God gives us; it's preparation for a future that only He can see. God will use the talents He has given us and what we have learned to stretch us further—sometimes out of our comfort zones. Following the unknown path God has prepared leads us to a greater obedience, obedience that helps us to learn more of Him. This newfound knowledge will ultimately lead to happiness and contentment.

All of us have talent; we can prepare ourselves and make the most of opportunities when they arise. Our greatest challenge is not the lack of opportunity to respond to God's leading, but being ready when opportunity comes.

Seek the Lord's face by prayer and study of His Word. Then hold on to His promises and trust in Him. When our focus is set on His face, we are open and ready to learn whatever He wants to teach us. We are prepared.

*Father, guide me on Your path to success. Help me to learn
of You and use what You teach me for Your glory. Amen.*

WHAT'S THIS THING IN MY EYE?

*"Why do you look at the speck of sawdust in your brother's
eye and pay no attention to the plank in your own eye?"*
LUKE 6:41 NIV

Whether we admit it or not, we judge others. Maybe it's how they look ("Just how many tattoos does a person need?") or their political leaning ("How can you call yourself a Christian and vote for a president from *that* party?"). Sometimes we pigeonhole others because of an accent ("What an ignorant hillbilly!") or an achievement of some kind ("Mr. Smarty Pants thinks he's better than everyone else because of his PhD.")

Our Father God urges us not to judge others in this way. After all, He doesn't look at our outward appearance. He doesn't pay attention to our political affiliation or anything else in our lives that is open to interpretation. He looks at the heart and judges by whether we have a personal relationship with Him.

In Luke 6:41, Jesus reminds us through His sawdust/plank analogy that none of us are blameless. It's important to put our own shortcomings into perspective when we face the temptation to judge others. Today, work on removing the plank from your eye and praise God for His gift of grace!

*God, please forgive me for the times I have judged
others. Help me to develop a gentle spirit that can share
Your love and hope in a nonjudgmental way. Amen.*

FOLLOW THE LORD'S FOOTSTEPS

"Come, follow me," Jesus said,
"and I will send you out to fish for people."
MATTHEW 4:19 NIV

The beach was empty except for one lone walker near the water's edge. With every step she took, her feet left an impression in the sand. But as the waves lapped upon the shore, her footprints quickly vanished. Following her footsteps would have been impossible unless someone were walking close behind.

Jesus asked His disciples to follow Him, and He asks us to do the same. It sounds simple, but following Jesus can be a challenge. Sometimes we become impatient, not wanting to wait upon the Lord. We run ahead of Him by taking matters into our own hands and making decisions without consulting Him first. Or perhaps we aren't diligent to keep in step with Him. We fall behind, and soon Jesus seems so far away.

Following Jesus requires staying right on His heels. We need to be close enough to hear His whisper. Stay close to His heart by opening the Bible daily. Allow His Word to speak to your heart and give you direction. Throughout the day, offer up prayers for guidance and wisdom. Keep in step with Him, and His close presence will bless you beyond measure.

Dear Lord, grant me the desire to follow You.
Help me not to run ahead or lag behind. Amen.

....

....

....

....

....

....

....

....

IDOLATRY

The idols of the heathen are silver and gold, the work of men's hands.
They have mouths, but they speak not; eyes have they, but they see not; they
have ears, but they hear not; neither is there any breath in their mouths. They
that make them are like unto them: so is every one that trusteth in them.

<small>PSALM 135:15–18 KJV</small>

We use the word *idol* loosely in modern life, referring not to golden statues, but to celebrities or people we admire. Yet real idolatry is a serious matter. Wealth, beauty, power, freedom, control, or security can become idols to us.

Idols can be made from good things like relationships, families, religion, or work. When the psalmist says our idols are the work of our hands, he is telling us to look at our own lives, the things we spend our time, energy, thoughts, and resources to achieve. Anything we love and desire more than Christ becomes an idol.

Idols cannot speak transforming words to us. They can't see all that happens to us, past, present, and future, and they can't hear our cries for help. The psalmist warns us that those who spend themselves to make idols will become like them, powerless and lifeless.

Spend time in prayer and ask God to reveal any powerless idols you serve.

Gentle Savior, who died to set me free, please
show me the things I love more than You. Amen.

ANNUAL OR PERENNIAL?

They are like trees planted along the riverbank,
bearing fruit each season. Their leaves never wither,
and they prosper in all they do.
PSALM 1:3 NLT

Emily and Lisa had a lot in common, but their gardening preference was not one of them. Every spring, Emily ran to the garden center at her local home improvement store to purchase cartloads of beautiful flowers. Soon her yard would be a riot of color—from daisies to zinnias and everything in between.

While Emily was busy at the home improvement store, Lisa patiently waited. The majority of her planting had been done in the fall and in prior years, so each spring she simply waited. Nothing inspired hope in Lisa like the little green shoots poking their heads out of ground that had been cold for far too long.

Annuals or perennials? Each has its advantages. Annuals are inexpensive, provide instant gratification, and keep boredom from setting in. Perennials require an initial investment, but when properly tended, provide beauty year after year—long after the annuals have dried up and withered away. What's more, perennials generally become fuller and more lush with each year of growth. Perennials are designed for the long haul—not just short-term enjoyment but long-term beauty.

The application to our lives is two-fold. First, be a perennial—long-lasting, enduring, slow-growing, steady, and faithful. Second, don't be discouraged by your inevitable dormant seasons. Tend to your soul, and it will reward you with years of lush blossoms.

Father, be the gardener of my soul. Amen.

CHOOSE

*"But if serving the L*ORD* seems undesirable to you,*
then choose for yourselves this day whom you will serve. . . .
*But as for me and my household, we will serve the L*ORD*."*
JOSHUA 24:15 NIV

Under God's mighty hand, Joshua led the Israelites into the Promised Land. Toward the end of his life, he assembled the people together and shared the story of the Lord's deliverance. Then he laid out the choice that was before them. Joshua set an example by emphatically proclaiming his allegiance to the Lord.

We, too, must choose whom we will serve. The truth is, we all serve some-thing. We may serve careers, money, appearance, or even relationships. Although we may not admit it, we become slaves to whatever we choose to serve. Jesus warns us in Matthew 6:24 that we cannot serve two masters. We will hate the one and love the other, or we will be devoted to the one and despise the other. Here Jesus was referring to money, but our idol could be anything.

Who or what captivates your thoughts, motivates your actions, or inspires your passions? Whom do you love with all your heart, soul, mind, and strength? What has your heart's allegiance?

Let's get more specific. What keeps you from attending church? What gets in the way of reading the Bible? What prevents you from obeying the Lord? The answer to these difficult questions reveals what we have chosen to serve. Let's follow Joshua's example by choosing to serve the Lord with all we have!

Dear Lord, forgive me for choosing
to serve anything other than You.
Help me to faithfully love You. Amen.

FIRST THINGS FIRST

*Before daybreak the next morning, Jesus got
up and went out to an isolated place to pray.*
MARK 1:35 NLT

Jana was packing an overnight bag for a weekend trip. It didn't seem like she had that much stuff, but as hard as she tried, she just couldn't fit everything into the luggage. Finally her roommate, Lisa, came to the rescue. Within minutes, Lisa had the bag packed and ready to go.

"How on earth did you do that?" Jana asked, amazed at her efficiency.

"Simple," Lisa replied, "I just put the big things in first. Once the larger items are in place, it's much easier to stick the small things in the space that's left. You just have to start with the big stuff."

This concept works for our lives as well, and no one modeled this better than Jesus during His earthly ministry. His days were packed with urgency—no matter where He was or what He did, someone wanted something from Him. And yet He never seemed to be in a hurry and always accomplished everything that needed to be done. His secret? Jesus' priorities were clearly in order. He did the important things—like spending time with His Father—first.

If you're having trouble fitting everything into your life, take a moment to unpack your bag and reassess your priorities. Do the big things first, and everything else will fall into place.

*Father, there's no denying that I'm busy and there's much
to be done. Order my priorities; help me to put You first
and trust You to help me do the rest. Amen.*

GODLY BEAUTY

*Like a gold ring in a pig's snout is a
beautiful woman who shows no discretion.*
PROVERBS 11:22 NIV

Today's society has redefined beauty, and it certainly does not include discretion. There is nothing discreet about the advertisements for sexy lingerie we see in magazines and even on television during prime time.

Some of the most attractive female stars fail to use discretion in their choices regarding their apparel, child-rearing, materialism, drugs, and relationships with men. Yet these women are teenage girls' role models. What happened to "pretty is as pretty does?" What happened to modesty?

We are called to honor the Lord by demonstrating discretion. In doing so, we also guard our hearts. The Bible calls the heart the "wellspring of life." It is difficult to live a pure life for Jesus while lacking modesty in choices of clothing, language, and lifestyle.

A gold ring is a thing of beauty, but in a pig's snout, it quickly loses its appeal! A beautiful woman without discretion may attract a crowd, but not the right one. She will receive attention, but in the form of shock rather than respect.

As a Christian woman, no matter your shape or size, height or hair color, you are *beautiful*. Beauty is in the heart first. It shines forth through attitudes and actions that honor God. This is true beauty.

*Lord, when I am tempted to use beauty to attract
the world to my body, remind me that a godly woman
uses modesty to point the world to You. Amen.*

A NEW PERSPECTIVE

But do not forget this one thing, dear friends:
With the Lord a day is like a thousand years,
and a thousand years are like a day.

2 PETER 3:8 NIV

Imagine that your workday was five minutes long. You'd hardly have time to clock in and get settled at your desk. You'd maybe have a minute or two to check email, and suddenly the day would be over. The time would fly.

But what if you spent five minutes sitting at a stoplight? It would seem like an eternity. Five minutes can fly by, or it can drag on forever. It all depends on your perspective.

For Jonah, spending a few nights in the belly of a fish changed his perspective from doing whatever he could to avoid God to doing whatever he could to follow Him obediently. For Job, losing everything changed his perspective from enjoying life's luxuries to falling on his knees and begging God to deliver him. For Saul, a blinding light changed his perspective from investing his life in hunting down Christians to pouring out his life at the foot of the cross.

If you are feeling worried, burdened, or overwhelmed, take a step back and look at the big picture. Ask God to give you some of His perspective. Maintaining a biblical perspective on our circumstances can mean the difference between peace and anxiety, between sorrow and joy.

Father, I admit that I often become discouraged by
my circumstances. Please give me a fresh perspective
and help me to see my life through Your eyes. Amen.

....

....

....

....

....

....

SPRING CLEANING

Purify me from my sins, and I will be clean;
wash me, and I will be whiter than snow.
PSALM 51:7 NLT

Traditionally the time when snow melts and daffodils bloom is when we turn our thoughts toward spring cleaning. Women of old would hang the quilts outside to air, throw the rugs over the fence to beat out the dust, wash the ceilings and walls to remove traces of wood and coal smoke, and tackle a never-ending list of necessary springtime chores.

Today our homes are more efficient and don't require quite as heavy a cleaning each spring, but we still tend to cull out the clutter of too much stuff and redecorate to refresh our environment.

When we look within our heart, we can always see places where a good annual cleaning is in order. In the dark corners of the heart are dust bunnies of envy and fear. On the floor and furniture is the clutter of stress and strife. Hanging from the ceiling are cobwebs of worry and confusion. Buried and forgotten under all that is the joy and peace God intended for us to enjoy in life.

Though it takes time, focus, and sometimes a bit of pain, a spiritual inventory is well worth the effort to lighten our burdens and refresh our outlook.

Dear Lord, help me to take the necessary time to do
some spiritual housecleaning. Help me to sweep out
the collection of junk so my soul is renewed. Amen.

CHRIST, OUR SANCTUARY

O God, thou art my God; early will I seek thee: my soul thirsteth for thee,
my flesh longeth for thee in a dry and thirsty land, where no water is; to see
thy power and thy glory, so as I have seen thee in the sanctuary.
PSALM 63:1-2 KJV

The word *sanctuary* may make you think of a church, an altar, a place of quiet beauty, a place to worship. You may also think of a place of rest and safety where animals may live protected. At various times in history, a sanctuary was a place of refuge where even accused criminals could seek shelter.

Christ Himself is our sanctuary. The psalmist speaks of hungering and thirsting, both body and soul. What is he looking for? He is searching for God. Clearly he did not find salvation in the dry, thirsty land where there was no water, and neither will we. The world's offerings, counsel, and substances have nothing to sustain us. Satisfaction can only be found in relationship with Jesus Christ, the One who called Himself living water and bread of life. The power and glory of God are manifest in Him. In Matthew 11:28 Jesus tells us to come to Him and we will find rest for our souls. Christ Himself is the sanctuary, the place of rest, protection, and shelter.

Lord Jesus, forgive me for seeking rest
and satisfaction in the desert of this world.
Thank You for being my sanctuary. Amen.

....
....
....
....
....
....
....

WHEN I THINK OF THE HEAVENS

When I consider your heavens, the work of
your fingers, the moon and the stars, which you
have set in place, what is mankind, that you are mindful
of them, human beings that you care for them?

PSALM 8:3–4 NIV

Do you ever spend time thinking about the vastness of God? His greatness? His majesty? When you ponder His creation—the heavens, the moon, and the stars—do you feel tiny in comparison? Do you wonder how, in the midst of such greatness, He even remembers your name, let alone the details of your life or the problems you go through?

Daughter of God, you are important to your heavenly Father, more important than the sun, the moon, and the stars. You are created in the image of God, and He cares for you. In fact, He cares so much that He sent His Son, Jesus, to offer His life as a sacrifice for your sins.

The next time you look up at the heavens, the next time you *ooh* and *aah* over a majestic mountain or emerald waves crashing against a shoreline, remember that those things, in all their splendor, don't even come close to you—God's greatest creation.

Oh Father, when I look at everything You have created,
I'm so overwhelmed with who You are. Who am I that You
would think twice about me? And yet You do. You love me,
and for that I'm eternally grateful! Amen.

ANXIETY CHECK!

Do not be anxious about anything,
but in every situation, by prayer and petition,
with thanksgiving, present your requests to God.
PHILIPPIANS 4:6 NIV

Twenty-first-century women are always checking things. A bank balance. Email. Voice mail. The grocery list. And, of course, that never-ending to-do list. We routinely get our oil, tires, and brake fluid checked. And we wouldn't think of leaving home for the day without checking our appearance in the mirror. We even double-check our purses, making sure we have the essentials—lipstick, mascara, and the cell phone.

Yes, checking is a part of living, isn't it? We do it without even realizing it. Checking to make sure we've locked the door, turned off the stove, and unplugged the curling iron just comes naturally. So why do we forget some of the bigger checks in life? Take anxiety, for instance.

When was the last time you did an anxiety check? Days? Weeks? Months? Chances are, you're due for another. After all, we're instructed not to be anxious about anything. Instead, we're to present our requests to God with thanksgiving in our hearts. We're to turn to Him in prayer so He can take our burdens. Once they've lifted, it's bye-bye anxiety!

Father, I get anxious sometimes. And I don't always remember to turn to You
with my anxiety. In fact, I forget to check for anxiety at all. Today I hand my
anxieties to You. Thank You that I can present my requests to You. Amen.

APPROVAL TRAP

*Those who flatter their neighbors
are spreading nets for their feet.*
PROVERBS 29:5 NIV

We all want to be liked. It is human nature to want validation, especially from those we love and respect. There is a trap, though, in loving the praise of others. Needing to have the approval of people can become a form of idolatry. When this happens, we lose the freedom Jesus intends for us. We make choices based on what another person will say or think about us. We begin to live our lives for the applause and praise of others. Often we compromise whom we are and some of the things we should be doing in life.

When you are assured that God loves you and accepts you in Christ no matter what you have done, you will not need the praise of others. You may sometimes get worldly praise—and you may receive it graciously—but you will not need it because your security rests firmly in your approval from God Himself.

*Lord, thank You for accepting me and forgiving all my sins.
Show me if I have become a slave to others' opinions of me
and help me to be free of the need for their approval. Amen.*

THE POWER OF THE WORD

Heaven and earth shall pass away:
but my words shall not pass away.

LUKE 21:33 KJV

Every word spoken about Jesus by the Old Testament prophets was fulfilled. Every word that Jesus uttered when He lived on earth was true and powerful. The gospel of John tells us He *is* the Living Word of God.

When God's Word is planted in our lives it can transform us, choking out weeds of distraction, indifference, and unbelief. Because Jesus lives, every word spoken by Him has power today. By the Holy Spirit, God's words can accomplish His will in our lives, just as they did when Jesus spoke to those around Him when He walked on the earth.

Pray for a desire to read the Word and for memory to call it to mind when you need it. Ask God to sink the Word deep in the soil of your heart. Pray to see the transforming power of the Word in your life. Set aside time daily to read the Bible and pray, then watch and see God's faithfulness to work His Word into your life.

Lord Jesus, I have forgotten the power of Your Word
and have trusted other things more than You. Give me
a desire to read and hear Your Word and obey Your
voice. Thank You for what You will do in my life. Amen.

A STRONG HEART

*Whom have I in heaven but you? And earth has nothing
I desire besides you. My flesh and my heart may fail,
but God is the strength of my heart and my portion forever.*
PSALM 73:25–26 NIV

Do you ever feel like you have a weak heart? Like you're not strong? You cave at every little thing? Do you face life's challenges with your emotions in turmoil instead of facing them head-on with courage and strength? If so, you're not alone. Twenty-first century women are told they can "be it all" and "do it all," but it's not true. God never meant for us to be strong every moment of our lives. If we were, we wouldn't need Him.

Here's the good news: You don't have to be strong. In your weakness, God's strength shines through. And His strength surpasses anything you could produce, even on your best day. It's the same strength that spoke the heavens and the earth into existence. The same strength that parted the Red Sea. And it's the same strength that made the journey up the hill to the cross.

So how do you tap into that strength? There's really only one way. Come into His presence. Spend some quiet time with Him. Acknowledge your weakness, then allow His strong arms to encompass you. There's really nothing else in heaven or on earth to compare. God is all you will ever need.

*Father, I feel so weak at times. It's hard just to put one
foot in front of the other. But I know You are my strength.
Invigorate me with that strength today, Lord. Amen.*

GREEN PASTURES

He maketh me to lie down in green pastures:
he leadeth me beside the still waters.

PSALM 23:2 KJV

Perhaps today's verse brings to mind images of reclining alongside a mountain stream or resting in an open field. Maybe if you close your eyes you can almost hear the sound of water rushing against the rocks in the creek bed or smell the sweetness of the grass. What a perfect place to meet with God, in the quiet stillness.

Have you ever considered that the Lord "makes" us lie down in green pastures? The verse doesn't say He "leads" us to green pastures, or even that He "hopes" we'll lie down in green pastures. No, it's clear. He *makes* us lie down. But why? What's so important about our quiet time with Him? And if it's truly important, why don't we just do it on our own?

Twenty-first-century women lead busy lives. There's so much to get done, and so little time to do it. Our intentions are good; we intend to meet with God, but we forget. Or we get busy. Or we meet with Him and then get distracted.

When life is at its most chaotic, don't be surprised if God makes you lie down in green pastures. He will woo you from the busyness to rest by a quiet stream . . .so He can have you all to Himself.

Lord, I don't often meet You at the quiet streams.
More often than not, I have a quick word with You
in the car on my way to work. Today, I commit to meet
You in green pastures, to rest at Your feet. Amen.

GOING ABOVE AND BEYOND

Now to him who is able to do immeasurably more than all we ask or imagine,
according to his power that is at work within us, to him be glory in the church
and in Christ Jesus throughout all generations, for ever and ever!
EPHESIANS 3:20–21 NIV

Are you one of those people who goes above and beyond—at work, in your relationships, and at play? Maybe you like to do all you've promised to do, and then some. If this is true of you, then you're more like your heavenly Father than you know. His Word promises that He always goes above and beyond all that we could ask or imagine.

Think about that for a moment. What have you asked for? What have you imagined? It's amazing to think that God, in His infinite power and wisdom, can do immeasurably more than all that! How? According to the power that is at work within us. It's not our power, thankfully. We don't have enough power to scrape the surface of what we'd like to see done in our lives. But His power in us gets the job done. . .and more.

Praise the Lord! Praise Him in the church and throughout all generations! He's an immeasurable God.

Heavenly Father, I feel pretty powerless at times. It's amazing to
realize You have more power in Your little finger than all of mankind
has put together. Today I praise You for being a God who goes
above and beyond all I could ask or imagine. Amen.

A FAMILY BLESSING

*And now, may it please you to bless the house of your servant, so that it may
continue forever before you. For you have spoken, and when you grant a
blessing to your servant, O Sovereign LORD, it is an eternal blessing!*

2 SAMUEL 7:29 NLT

God is completely trustworthy. Think about that for a moment. When we can't
trust others, we can trust Him. When we can't trust ourselves, we can trust
Him. God keeps an eye on everyone at all times. He's got things under control,
especially when we loosen our grip.

Did you know that you can trust God with both your own life *and* the lives
of your family members? And that includes every single person in your family.
Parents, grandparents, siblings, children, aunts, uncles—everyone. You can trust
the Lord with their dreams, their goals, their aspirations, their attitudes, their
reactions, their problems. You can trust Him to handle any relationship problems.
God's got it covered. All of it.

Today, recommit yourself to trusting God with your family. Don't fret and
don't try to fix people. That's not your job, after all. And besides, God's keeping
an eye on everyone. He's said it, and you can believe it. It's in His master plan
to bless your family. . .permanently!

*God, I confess I sometimes struggle where my family is
concerned. I want to fix people. I want to fix situations.
Thank You for the reminder that You have great plans,
not just for me, but for my family members too. Amen.*

WRONG MESSAGES

"They are not of the world,
even as I am not of the world."
JOHN 17:16 NASB

The world sends women messages every day. You should be thin with long, flowing, gorgeous hair. You should be married to a man—tall, dark, and handsome, of course—and on your ring finger there should be a sparkling diamond. You should smell of the finest, most expensive perfume. And if you are to be loved, you should dress a certain way, talk a certain way, and live in a certain neighborhood.

But believers in Christ are not of this world. We are *in* it, but not *of* it. We are visitors here, and heaven will be our eternal home. While we are here on earth, we must avoid believing the things the world whispers to us. It is okay if you are not beautiful in the world's eyes. God sees you as a beautiful daughter, important enough to give His Son's life for! Diamonds and perfume are not the definition of a woman. It is the heart that defines her, and if her heart is turned toward Jesus, it will shine brighter than any diamond ever could.

Father, remind me today to tune out the world as
I tune into what You have to say about me. Amen.

DOING OUR PART

*Therefore, my dear friends, as you have always obeyed—
not only in my presence, but now much more in my
absence—continue to work out your salvation with fear
and trembling, for it is God who works in you to will
and to act in order to fulfill his good purpose.*

PHILIPPIANS 2:12–13 NIV

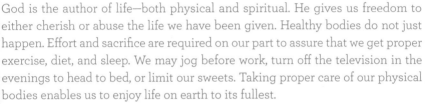

God is the author of life—both physical and spiritual. He gives us freedom to either cherish or abuse the life we have been given. Healthy bodies do not just happen. Effort and sacrifice are required on our part to assure that we get proper exercise, diet, and sleep. We may jog before work, turn off the television in the evenings to head to bed, or limit our sweets. Taking proper care of our physical bodies enables us to enjoy life on earth to its fullest.

In the same way, we must make the effort to maintain optimal spiritual health. Spiritual growth doesn't just happen—it takes a lot of discipline. Obedience is required. Reading God's Word is a great start, but we must take it a step further. We need to transfer our head knowledge to the heart by applying God's truth in everyday life.

The good news is that we're not alone in our pursuit of spiritual health. Along the way, the Holy Spirit gives us the desire and ability to follow the Lord. Let's not forget that spiritual growth is not only profitable for this life, but for the life to come!

*Dear Lord, may I obediently apply Your truth to my daily life.
Thank You for helping me in this process. Amen.*

THE WORKER'S TOIL

What do workers gain from their toil? I have
seen the burden God has laid on the human race.
He has made everything beautiful in its time.
ECCLESIASTES 3:9–11 NIV

Most women are hard workers. They spend hours a day either caring for the needs of others or working at their jobs. They give tirelessly of themselves and come home at the end of the day worn out. There's not always much energy left over to effectively develop a relationship with the Lord.

If you're the type of woman who works especially hard, you might wonder if you'll ever find the beauty in your labors. Perhaps it all seems to be in vain—for someone else's benefit. Take heart! Work is a necessity, but it doesn't have to consume you. Be on the lookout for telltale signs that you're working too hard. If your prayer time is suffering or you don't feel as close to the Lord as you once did, it might be time to reorganize your schedule.

Keeping things in balance is key. Hard work is good—and so is rest. And if you're so taxed that you're not effective, then it's definitely time for a change. Take a look at what drives you to work so hard. Then, as you are able, work with the Lord to bring every area of your life into perfect balance.

Lord, I sometimes think my life is out of balance.
I work too hard, then seem to crash. My down times
are too down. Bring order to my life, Father. Help me
to keep everything in perfect balance. Amen.

JUST ONE

One of them, when he saw he was healed,
came back, praising God in a loud voice.

LUKE 17:15 NIV

Ten men were afflicted with the horrible disease of leprosy. Ten met Jesus as He passed through their village. Ten called out, addressing Him by name, "Jesus, Master, have pity on us!" Ten received healing from the Lord.

There were ten men that day, but then in a moment's time there was but one. One man rushed back and threw himself at the feet of Jesus. He used the same loud voice that had pled for mercy to offer thankfulness and praise.

We read this passage, and we want to shake our heads at those other nine. How could they have forgotten to thank Jesus? They had just been healed of leprosy! How could they go on about their day, not honoring Him with gratitude?

Before we judge too harshly, we must examine our own hearts. Do we remember to thank God when a prayer is answered?

Do you give Him glory for answering your prayers for a friend's marriage to be restored, or do you merely comment that it's great the couple has decided to reunite? Do you thank Him for providing a new job after your Bible study group prayed on your behalf? Or are you too busy picking out the suit and heels you will wear on your first day?

It takes discipline to react like the one leper rather than like the other nine. God delights when He finds a believer with a grateful heart.

Help me, Lord, to have a grateful heart. Amen.

CHANGING HEARTS

*In the Lord's hand the king's heart is a stream of
water that he channels toward all who please him.*

PROVERBS 21:1 NIV

Relationships can be difficult at times. Even when communication is good and both people are Christians, there is still conflict when two human beings have a long-term relationship with each other. Children, parents, coworkers, roommates, friends, sisters, former spouses, and in-laws can all frustrate us at one time or another. We have our own desires and goals we want to meet; they have their agendas and needs, and everyone has selfishness in his or her heart. How do we get beyond competing desires that conflict with each other and harm our relationships?

Prayer is a key ingredient in pursuing successful relationships. We can pray for our own hearts to change as well as those we're in conflict with. God can and will shape our affections, and He can change the minds of those for whom we pray. It is not difficult for Him, yet we so easily forget to ask. What relationships in your life need prayer today?

*Heavenly Father, there is nothing in my heart and
mind or in those of whom I love that You cannot change.
Turn my heart to You to desire Your best for my life. Amen.*

....

....

....

....

....

....

....

M.I.A.?

Why, LORD, do you stand far off?
Why do you hide yourself in times of trouble?
PSALM 10:1 NIV

Do you ever feel like God is Missing in Action? Like He's hard to reach during the very times you need Him most? Have you ever wondered if the Lord is actually avoiding you during your times of crisis? If He even cares at all about what you're going through?

God isn't in the avoiding business. And He cares about you very much. In fact, He loves you deeply and is with you through thick and thin. If you're in a season in which His voice seems to be waning, take the time to listen more attentively. If you still can't hear His voice, remember there are times when He chooses to remain silent. That doesn't mean He's not there or that He doesn't care. Nothing could be further from the truth. Perhaps He's just waiting to see if you're going to act out of what you already know, what He's already taught you.

If God's voice isn't clear right now, think back to the last thing you heard Him speak to your heart. Act on it. Just keep walking in consistent faith, love, and hope. Before long, you'll be hearing His voice again. . .crystal clear.

Lord, I'm calling out to You today. Sometimes I feel like You're
not there. Until I hear Your voice, I'm going to keep on believing,
keep on hoping, and keep on living a life of faith. Amen.

THE WRESTLING MATCH

How long must I wrestle with my thoughts
and day after day have sorrow in my heart?
How long will my enemy triumph over me?
PSALM 13:2 NIV

Every day we struggle with thoughts that may not be pleasing to God. Not everything that flits through our mind or imagination is edifying to Him, after all. And it's frustrating to know we fall short of where we think we should be, especially when it comes to what we think or feel.

When we struggle in our thought life, the enemy is thrilled. But he needs to take a second look. Those fleeting thoughts are not sinful unless we act on them. And if we can stop them while they're just thoughts—if we can bring them under the blood of Jesus—then the battle is already won! Satan may be gleeful now, but when we recognize that we are conquerors through Christ, he stops partying and is vanquished.

Your mind is the battlefield. That's why we are advised to bring every thought captive, because the enemy will try to defeat us in our mind before actions ever come into play. Instead of wrestling with your thoughts, make a conscious effort to give your thought life to the One capable of handling it.

Father, sometimes I don't like the thoughts that flit through my mind.
I know they're not Your thoughts. Today, I give my thought life to You.
May the enemy no longer triumph over me in this area! Amen.

A STREAM RUNS THROUGH

He that believeth on me, as the scripture hath said,
out of his belly shall flow rivers of living water.
JOHN 7:38 KJV

Water from the sprinkler arced through the air, casting drops over the grass. Only when it slapped a large oak did it lose its trajectory and dribble to the ground. The water couldn't pass through the oak tree. Yes, the thirsty tree soaked up the needed moisture, but it stopped the shooting sprays.

Do we stop the life-giving water of the Savior from gushing out of our hearts? Is a large oak tree—maybe fear, doubt, anger—rooted within us that keeps the flow of water stilled?

Jesus encouraged us to believe in Him so there would be an overflowing of the Spirit upon others. If we harbor destructive emotions, the Spirit is slapping the oak tree. It's not flowing out of us. While our circumstances might not be perfect, we're still asked to let the river flow.

The Spirit within us is greater than any trouble we might face, any situation we might be in, any obstacle in our paths. We need to acknowledge His promise and obey His commands so God can work in our lives. When we do, streams of water flow.

Dear heavenly Father, help me to ferret out
anything that would keep the Holy Spirit from
working in my life. Thank You, Lord. Amen.

BECOME A WORLD-CHANGING WOMAN

"This is my command—be strong and courageous!
*Do not be afraid or discouraged. For the L*ORD
your God is with you wherever you go."
JOSHUA 1:9 NLT

In the Word of God, women from all professions and backgrounds are changed by grace, and then, with the Holy Spirit's help, transform the people around them. In the Old Testament, God shines the light on a beauty queen (Esther) who saves an entire generation of people with her bravery. In Exodus, Moses' sister Miriam, exhorts her fellow Israelites to worship. And in the New Testament, Lydia and Tabitha run successful businesses and invest their profits in ministry to the poor.

God wants you to change your world, too. Does that thought scare you? Whatever station God has called you to, He will equip you for the task. Are you a businesswoman? He will guide you to do your job with integrity and faithfulness. Do you have a classroom of kids looking up to you? God will give you energy and creativity to discipline, lead, and teach them. Perhaps you've felt called to minister, and wonder whether you've heard God right. Through circumstances, scripture, and mature Christian mentors, He will make clear the path He wants you to take.

Don't be afraid to follow God—wherever He leads. Women in every era have changed the world because they remained faithful to God and followed His leadership.

Lord, help me be strong and courageous as
I follow You wherever You lead. I want You
to use me to help change the world. Amen.

HANDS THAT HOLD

*My times are in your hands; deliver me from the
hands of my enemies, from those who pursue me.*

PSALM 31:15 NIV

Our lives are composed of seconds, minutes, hours, days, weeks, months, and years. We think in each of these increments in different situations. Look at a clock and we think about seconds, minutes, and hours. Our calendar shows us days, weeks, and months. On a birthday or holiday, we reflect on a year. We may think about the era in which we live and the culture around us that inhabits that time frame. We may dwell too much in the past or worry too much about our future. All of these are part of the times that the psalmist places in God's hands.

Think about God's hands that hold our time. These are the hands that fashioned the world. These are the hands that took a rib from Adam and made Eve. These are the hands that healed the blind and the lame. These are the hands that broke bread in an upper room. These are the hands that were nailed to a cross. These are the hands graciously extended to doubting Thomas. Our times, from our moments to our years, are in the hands of the Creator, Healer, Sustainer, Provider, Redeemer, and Lover of our souls. There is nothing He cannot do. Knowing this, the psalmist releases his fears to God—so can you.

*Gracious God who rules and reigns over all my days,
cause me to remember that I am held by Your loving
hands and you will never let me go. Amen.*

TAKING MATTERS INTO
HER OWN HANDS

But the Lord's plans stand firm forever;
his intentions can never be shaken.
PSALM 33:11 NLT

Genesis 27 tells the story of Jacob, Esau, and their meddling mother, Rebekah. This mother was so concerned for her son's future that she took matters into her own hands.

An ailing Isaac instructed Esau to prepare a meal for him so that Esau could receive the blessing reserved for the firstborn son. Rebekah overheard this conversation and quickly hatched a new plan for younger son Jacob to receive the blessing. Rebekah's plan worked, and before Esau returned from his hunt, Jacob had stolen his brother's blessing. Although Romans 9:11 says this was God's plan all along, Rebekah's interference drove a potentially deadly wedge between her two grown sons.

Are you ever impatient for God's plans to unfold? Are you ever tempted to take matters into your own hands and act in a manipulative way? Sometimes this works and our plans succeed, just like Rebekah's. However, when we do this, the consequences can often be disastrous. Learn to wait on God. You can be assured that His plans and purposes will be fulfilled. And His way is always the best way.

Thank You, Father, that Your plans stand firm, even when I try to
intervene. Help me to wait patiently on You and to trust You to
bring about Your plans in Your way and in Your time. Amen.

SELF-SACRIFICE, NOT SELF-HELP

Then Jesus said to his disciples. . . . If you want
to save your life, you will destroy it. But if you
give up your life for me, you will find it.
MATTHEW 16:24–25 CEV

Every so often, a self-help book captivates readers and soars onto bestseller lists. The text is usually a combination of common sense and New Age philosophy, with a few Bible verses thrown in for good measure. Its principles tout both good advice and bad, and its followers tend to become zealous about it. Sure, the book might have some merit, but it doesn't factor in God. And the scriptures say that anything not done with and for God is meaningless.

As Jesus told His disciples, anyone who intends to follow God must let Him lead. We can't make plans and ask God to bless them. Instead, we must accept Jesus' sacrifice, ask for His forgiveness and grace, and surrender ourselves to Him. In return, He will give us the Holy Spirit. The Spirit's presence gives us comfort, guidance, and the strength to follow Him. He will empower us to embrace self-sacrifice.

Do you want to achieve big things? Ask God for His guidance, and follow the instructions He reveals. After all, His idea of success might be very different from yours. The good news is this: His dreams for us are perfect, because He created us. And the future He has for us will truly satisfy our souls, as we become all He created us to be.

Lord, help me to learn and follow Your way,
through self-sacrifice and not self-help. Amen.

ANGER

Anger is an emotion that can cause great harm if we leave it unchecked. Anger can result in sin that affects us and the people around us. How do we take charge of this emotion and handle it appropriately?

Anger may arise in our hearts because someone has hurt us. The pain ignites a tiny spark of fire deep within. We may fan the flame by allowing our minds to dwell on the hurt. As we dredge up past offenses, we add fuel to the fire. Soon the tiny spark has become a raging fire in our souls looking for an outlet. We seek retaliation, even wanting to inflict pain on the attacker. We lash out with our tongues to pay back the offense. As we sin in our anger, Satan enters the picture.

God has a better plan. Rather than allowing the fire in your heart to spew from your tongue, take your hurt to the Lord before you speak. Confess your anger and ask Him to help you forgive. Forgiveness squelches anger like throwing cold water on a fire, and through forgiveness God is glorified in your life.

*Dear Lord, help me deal with anger when
it first arises in my heart. May I give You
a foothold by choosing forgiveness. Amen.*

LIVING GOD'S WORD

*Do not merely listen to the word, and so deceive yourselves.
Do what it says. Anyone who listens to the word but does
not do what it says is like someone who looks at his face in
a mirror and, after looking at himself, goes away
and immediately forgets what he looks like.*

JAMES 1:22–24 NIV

The Bible contains instructions, promises, and encouraging words. It also contains warnings such as this one in James. The Bible is just another book if we do not heed its teachings and apply them to our lives. If we claim to be Christians, we must take the Word of God seriously.

How does this play out in real life?

Each day, we are faced with situations that give us options. Some of our options are how to react when we are treated unfairly at work or when we get cut off by another driver in traffic. As you read God's Word, take time to consider how the passages and insights apply to your daily life. Do not merely read the words, but challenge yourself to *live* them. In doing so, your life will be blessed and your God will be honored.

*Father, I admit that many times I simply read the
Bible as if it were a storybook. Remind me to apply
its truths and commands to my life. Amen.*

LISTENING TO GOD

"Why do you spend money for what is not bread, and your wages
for what does not satisfy? Listen carefully to Me, and eat what is good,
and delight yourself in abundance. Incline your ear, and come to Me.
Listen, that you may live; and I will make an everlasting covenant
with you, according to the faithful mercies shown to David."

ISAIAH 55:2–3 NASB

Whom do you follow? Whom do you listen to? Celebrities and politicians? The mainstream media and pop culture? What messages do they give? Are you satisfied with their advice and promises?

This world and its counsel have nothing lasting to offer us. The culture's solutions are short-lived. The very thing we think we must have or do brings only a temporary satisfaction.

The Lord calls us to listen to only Him. "Incline your ear. Come. Hear," He says. Relationship with Him—the Bread of Life—is what nourishes and sustains us, what fills the emptiness inside us. He has the ability to delight our souls. Lasting joy and peace come from knowing we are loved unconditionally by Him.

Whose voice are you listening to today? Hear the voice of Jesus calling you to come to Him.

Lord Jesus, forgive me for following the
world's voice instead of Yours. Cause
me to listen and follow You. Amen.

YOU'RE CHUBBY

They can urge the younger women to love their
husbands and children, to be self-controlled and pure.
TITUS 2:4–5 NIV

As Dianne walked her niece to school, the six-year-old suddenly burst out with, "You're chubby," punctuated with a throaty giggle.

Dianne gulped and laughed back with, "Don't you want to grow up and have nice curves like me?"

"Nope," came the reply. "I don't want to get old. I want to stay young and skinny."

Dianne was speechless as they reached the elementary school steps and her niece skipped inside. She realized she had just missed a teachable moment, but—really—what should she have said?

Dianne knew her sister-in-law was trying to lose some baby fat to get into a new dress for a high school reunion. It wasn't a big deal—or was it? Was a six-year-old already forming a warped body image by watching her mother preen before a mirror like any other woman in her midthirties might do?

A recent survey of girls ages eleven to seventeen found that their number-one wish was not to own a horse or get on the cheerleading squad, but to lose weight. All women have a hand in shaping how these girls develop their body images. We are charged by God to protect their innocence and lead them to desire healthy bodies, minds, and souls.

Dear Lord, help me to reach out to a girl in my
circle of influence and teach her to see herself
as a beautiful creation of Yours, no matter
how the package is wrapped. Amen.

ONE WAY

*Jesus told him, "I am the way, the truth, and the life.
No one can come to the Father except through me."*
JOHN 14:6 NLT

Jenny had just finished reading the newest self-help bestseller—the one that all of Hollywood was raving about—and she couldn't help but be a little confused. The book focused on inner peace and happiness, and when it talked about God, the almighty Creator and heavenly Father that she knew seemed more like a mystical force that a person could experience through self-reflection and. . .well. . .just about anything else that someone wanted to try.

The truth is that there's only *one* way to the Father—through Jesus Christ. Since the dawn of time, humans have sought eagerly after other paths to God, but His Word spells it out plainly: Jesus is the way, the truth, and the life. Take comfort in knowing that an understanding Savior is the solitary way to the Creator. He's been here and opened the way to God, and He lives today at the right hand of the Father in heaven.

*Father, forgive me for seeking You in ways other than through
Jesus. I know in my heart that He is the way, the truth, and the life.
Give me the strength to share this fact with people around me
who are looking for answers in the wrong places. Amen.*

A HARD DAY'S NIGHT

*I am worn out from sobbing. All night I flood my
bed with weeping, drenching it with my tears.*

PSALM 6:6 NLT

Do you ever get sick and tired of being sick and tired? Fed up with being fed up? If so, then today's scripture verse surely rings true for you. Maybe you're going through a tough season. Unexpected challenges. Hard stuff. And maybe you think the night will never end.

Consider that only a God-focused heart recognizes when enough is enough. You've already made progress! Recognizing that you're ready to jump the hurdle is a good thing. But before you do, remember tears can have a positive effect. They're cleansing, after all. And being honest with yourself about your emotions is also a good thing as long as you can still affirm that God is good in the midst of your pain.

So cry for a season. Get it all out. Let the cleansing take place. Then when you reach that place where you know it's time to move on, get to it! Acknowledge your need for God, then get off that bed and back to work.

Father, I recognize that sometimes I need to cry. I just have to get things out. Thank You for giving me tears. They're a great release. Today, I give my tears and my fears to You. May I rise up off my bed, ready to face a new day! Amen.

SERVING OTHERS

*Love must be sincere. Hate what is evil;
cling to what is good. Be devoted to one another
in love. Honor one another above yourselves.*
ROMANS 12:9–10 NIV

As the pastor read the weekly announcements, Alex noticed a young mother come into the sanctuary for the first time. The mother was trying to hold her fussy toddler, a diaper bag, purse, and her Bible as she looked around for a place to sit.

Alex wasn't the scheduled greeter, but it was obvious that the mother was embarrassed. Quietly, she stood and approached the mother and toddler and offered to carry her belongings and help her find a seat. She let her know where the nursery was in case she'd like to take her toddler there. After church, she invited them to lunch and introduced the mother to other women in the church.

God calls us to react in everyday situations in such a way that we show Christ's love to others. When we put others' needs before our own, we please God.

*Dear God, thank You that You have called me to love others
with Your love. Show me how I may demonstrate Your love
in practical ways to those people I am near today. Amen.*

PONDERING

But Mary treasured all these things,
pondering them in her heart.

LUKE 2:19 NASB

Mary was a young woman when she was chosen by God to bear His Son, Jesus. She had a lot to think about in the following days and months—a visitation from an angel that told her she would conceive a child even though she was a virgin, what Joseph would think, and then giving birth in a stable with shepherds showing up in the middle of the night to see her newborn son. Yes, Mary was young. But she possessed a great deal of depth. The Bible tells us that she pondered all of these things in her heart.

Do all women ponder? It seems that we do. We think about the good and the bad in our lives. We get lost in daydreams. We lie awake at night wondering. We question our decisions at times and second-guess them occasionally. We imagine. We wonder. We think.

Take a few moments today to ponder the blessings God has given you. You may be in the midst of a mountaintop experience in your life, or you may find yourself in a deep valley of turmoil. Wherever you are, remember this and treasure it in your heart: God sent His one and only Son to die for you. Ponder that kind of love.

Father, today when I am tempted to dwell on
the troubles in my heart, help me instead
to focus on the treasures. Amen.

WHOM SHALL I FEAR?

The LORD is my light and my salvation; whom shall I fear?
The LORD is the defense of my life; whom shall I dread?

PSALM 27:1 NASB

If the tentacles of fear grip your heart today, rest assured the Lord is not causing it. He's the author of peace. Even knowing that, we often struggle with situations and circumstances that make us afraid. So, what's a Christian woman to do?

First of all, we need to call on the Lord to protect us with His mighty hand. After all, we're God's kids, and our Daddy watches over us. And if anyone messes with us, they'd better watch out!

Next we have to recognize there's a huge difference between being cautious and being fearful. We're wise to be the first, of course. But anything—or anyone— that causes us to fear needs to be examined.

So, what are you afraid of today? Being alone? Money problems? Issues with children? Health-related concerns? Career moves? Things that go bump in the night? Most of the things we worry about never come to pass. They're mostly shadowy "what ifs." But when God sweeps in with that heavenly flashlight of His, He brings everything to light. And seeing our problems in the light certainly makes them less scary.

God, I'm ready to hand my fear over to You. I want to be cautious,
Lord, but not fearful. You are the strength of my life.
I've got nothing—or no one—to be afraid of. Amen.

WHAT DO YOU TREASURE?

*"Do not store up for yourselves treasures on earth,
where moths and vermin destroy, and where thieves
break in and steal. But store up for yourselves treasures
in heaven, where moths and vermin do not destroy,
and where thieves do not break in and steal. For where
your treasure is, there your heart will be also."*

MATTHEW 6:19-21 NIV

Thankfully, Tessa was home and awake when the smoke detector sounded. Her heart raced as she screamed for her brother who, only moments before, had been in the shower. She never thought to grab anything as they raced for the door—her single thought was for her brother's safety. As they stood across the street arm in arm watching the firefighters battle the flames, Tessa sobbed. It wasn't about the stuff—she knew it could be replaced. She simply was overwhelmed with thanks that both of them made it out alive.

There's nothing like a close call with disaster to reveal to us what is really important. Many of us invest an inordinate amount of time, money, and energy in acquiring things, and yet if we're faced with having to choose between people and possessions, we would choose people every time. We find our hearts aren't really in material things after all. Often we're tempted to invest our resources in acquiring material goods—sometimes at the expense of relationships. Jesus turns this principle upside down when He challenges us to invest our lives in things no disaster can destroy.

*Father, give me a heart like Yours. Teach me to invest
my resources in matters of eternal significance. Amen.*

CONFIDENCE

*But thou, O Lᴏʀᴅ, art a God full of
compassion, and gracious, long suffering,
and plenteous in mercy and truth.*

Pꜱᴀʟᴍ 86:15 ᴋᴊᴠ

Most of us base our confidence in our own knowledge, skills, good looks, or natural abilities. The truth is, our confidence should be in our Father God, not in our own efforts and talents.

Self-confidence is typically tied to our feelings. We feel good when we think we have done well and bad when we think we have not measured up. We may think of God as a schoolteacher who grades us on our performance. But God does not reward us based on what we do or do not do. That is the world's way. God is our Redeemer, our Savior, and the One who sees us through the righteousness and person of Jesus Christ.

Compassion, grace, longsuffering, mercy, and truth—these are attributes of our God. Compassion is *undeserved* sympathy. Grace is an *unmerited* gift. Longsuffering is patience *beyond reasonable standards*. None of these gifts have to do with our performance—all come out of His extravagant love. We give God our need, sin, dependence, and weakness. He gives us help, forgiveness, power, and strength.

*Heavenly Father, thank You that I may exchange all my sin and
weakness for Your forgiveness and strength. Help me to be
confident in Your character, not my performance. Amen.*

FOUNTAIN OF GOD

For with You is the fountain of life.
PSALM 36:9 NASB

Fountains are objects of beauty. The dance of water is constant, but our eyes never see quite the same scene for more than a second. The sound of splashing water is soothing and relaxing. Fountains evoke thoughts of constancy and renewal, cleansing and refreshment. Fountains are also a needed source of water, the most essential element of life.

God is the source of life for all creation. All things begin and end in Him. His love is beyond the bounds of the heavens. His beauty is constant as we see Him through circumstances that come into our lives. Even if we're unfaithful, God's faithfulness remains. It does not run dry. Over and over, He comforts His people. Daily His mercy is new to us, like clean water bubbling up from a fountain.

When we see ourselves in Him—our very lives held in His—all of creation together belonging to, controlled, and preserved by Him, we gain perspective on whom we are and how much we are loved. As the psalmist says, "With you is the fountain of life."

Heavenly Father, how little I know of Your majesty and beauty.
Your creation speaks more love to me than I can possibly comprehend.
Show me more and more of how my life is hidden in Yours. Amen.

PEOPLE NEED THE LORD

When he saw the crowds, he had compassion
on them because they were confused and
helpless, like sheep without a shepherd.
MATTHEW 9:36 NLT

Look closely at the people around you. External appearances are deceptive. Beneath the forced smiles lie hearts that reveal a different story. Aimless. Wandering. Lost. Many people have no idea why they are here, what they are doing, and where they are going. Pain, fear, and anxiety are their constant companions. They are like sheep without a shepherd.

We need the Lord's eyes to see people's hearts. Then compassion will compel us to reach out. People need to know that they are loved unconditionally. They need to understand that God has a purpose for their lives. They need to realize that God can guide them along life's journey. They need the hope of eternal life and the assurance of a heavenly home. Putting it simply, people need the Lord.

We are all sheep in need of the Good Shepherd. Live your life before others with authenticity and humility. Allow them to see God's peace in times of trials, the Father's comfort in times of grief, the Savior's hope in times of uncertainty. Be real so you can point others to Christ. Reach out and introduce someone to the Good Shepherd.

Dear Lord, open my eyes to see the lost sheep around me. May I
be used to introduce them to You, the Good Shepherd. Amen.

....

....

....

....

....

....

KNOW YOURSELF

Incline Your ear, O Lord, and answer me;
for I am afflicted and needy.

PSALM 86:1 NASB

✽

"Poor and needy" is not a phrase we use to describe ourselves. In fact, it is the last thing we would want said about us. We'd never find it on the pages of a self-help book or hear it from talk-show gurus. Daily we try to watch what we eat, get our exercise, and count on our talents, skills, and experience to secure our future. Though Philippians 3:3 tells us to put no confidence in our own human effort, we rely on ourselves every day.

Proverbs 29:23 (NKJV) says, "A man's pride will bring him low, but the humble in spirit will retain honor." How do we retain a humble spirit when the world constantly tells us how great it is to be self-reliant?

One way is to acknowledge our poverty and neediness before our heavenly Father. We need Him, and we need Him to hear us. Regardless of what we accomplish in the world through our own efforts, ultimately all we have and each breath we draw is a gift from God. Take comfort in knowing His sustaining power in our lives is all we need.

Heavenly Father, help me to remember whom I am before You.
Enable me to see myself as You see me, and keep me mindful
of my constant dependence on You. Amen.

....

....

....

....

....

....

....

HAVING IT ALL

When the woman saw that the fruit of the tree
was good for food and pleasing to the eye, and also
desirable for gaining wisdom, she took some and ate it.
GENESIS 3:6 NIV

It wasn't called Paradise for nothing. Eve had it all. A secure home. Beautiful surroundings. Peace. An attentive man who longed for her companionship. Freedom to roam the garden and eat almost anything her heart desired. However, in spite of having the resources to fulfill all of her wants and needs, there was a nagging place of longing in Eve's soul. Satan saw this vulnerability and took advantage of the opportunity.

Of all the things Satan could have tempted Eve with, he chose food. While the fruit can be a metaphor for many things that might cause us to sin, it's interesting that he chose food. Eve was not physically hungry. She had plenty to eat. She was drawn to the fruit because it looked beautiful. She was drawn to it because she thought it might make her like God.

We sin for the same reasons. Like Eve, every time we exchange long-term fellowship with God for the short-term reward of a pleasurable (but sinful) experience, we are saying that something is better suited to meet our needs than God Himself. That's a lot of pressure to put on a person, place, or thing.

Don't be afraid of that longing in your soul. Identify and acknowledge it. Then realize that nothing on earth can satisfy it except God.

Father, You are enough. Help me to
be satisfied with You alone. Amen.

....

....

....

....

....

WHAT DO YOU LONG FOR?

What will you gain, if you own the whole world but destroy
yourself? What could you give to get back your soul?
MARK 8:36–37 CEV

What do you long for? Is it financial freedom or more vacation time? Do you long to be married? Maybe you want to own your own home or start a business.

More importantly, what are you willing to do to get what you long for? Some people will go to extremes to achieve their dreams. Sometime people lose their common sense as they chase after their desires: Anorexics give up their health in order to be thin. Sex addicts sacrifice their dignity—and much more—as they go after what they believe will fulfill them. Some women change their personalities to please men.

But as children of God, we are to trust in God's timing and His plan. We might plan and take steps to achieve our goals, but we shouldn't run ahead of God's leadership. And we should always filter our longings through the Word of God and the counsel of mature Christians.

If the thing you long for isn't happening, ask God what He wants to teach you through the waiting. Ask Him to reveal how to grow and mature in your faith during this time.

Lord, help me to want You more than I want anything else.
Teach me never to trade my soul for something temporary. Amen.

IT'S ALL HIM

*"For in him we live and
move and have our being."*
ACTS 17:28 NIV

It's our human nature to want to be self-reliant. After all, even as toddlers we're praised as being a "big girl" for feeding ourselves, picking up toys, and selecting our own outfits.

Just like so many other things in God's kingdom, His view of self-sufficiency is the exact opposite of the world's take on it. *"Rely on Me,"* He tells us. *"You can't make it through this life alone, and I don't want you to. Let Me take care of you."*

The Bible tells us that when we become a part of God's family, our lives are no longer our own—we are bought with the blood of Jesus (1 Corinthians 6:20). Our independent nature may resist this notion, but in reality, letting God take control gives us the freedom we're looking for that we don't get when we try to rely on ourselves.

Problems? Give them to the One who bought you. Persecuted? Let Him deal with it. Lonely? Run to Him for the comfort you need. Living life inside the love of God has amazing benefits! Give up your need for independence and control, and let Him do great things in the life you share with Him.

Father, teach me new ways to depend on You. My heart knows that You are waiting to bless me in immeasurable ways if only I trust in You. Take my life—all of it—and use it for Your great and perfect plan. Amen.

MARY'S STORY

When Jesus rose early on the first day of the week,
he appeared first to Mary Magdalene,
out of whom he had driven seven demons.
MARK 16:9 NIV

Mary Magdalene was once was filled with demons—seven, to be exact. This woman knew great affliction, confusion, and grief. To go to bed each night and rise again each morning with strong demonic forces at work within her spirit must have been a miserable existence.

Then Mary of Magdala met Jesus of Nazareth, the One called the Messiah. He drove out the demons that had ruled her life, and she was never the same again. She became a part of Christ's inner circle of supporters. Mary Magdalene was a witness at His crucifixion and His burial. She saw the empty tomb, and she was the first person the risen Lord appeared to after His resurrection.

Perhaps you think your salvation story is not as exciting as Mary's. You walked an aisle at church in second grade and accepted Christ. You met Jesus at a Christian camp or through a relative. But truly, *every* story of salvation is exciting! However and whenever Jesus saved you, your story is powerful. Never think it less meaningful than another's. Our testimonies are meant to be shared!

Do you know Jesus? If so, will you be a modern-day Mary? The world needs passionate believers in Jesus. The world needs to know about the Messiah. Don't keep Him a secret.

Father, give me courage to share my testimony
with someone who needs to know You. Amen.

STRENGTH IN WEAKNESS

This is what the Sovereign LORD, the Holy One of Israel says:
"Only in returning to me and resting in me will you be saved.
In quietness and confidence is your strength."
ISAIAH 30:15 NLT

Assert yourself, work hard, make progress, speak up, and believe in yourself. These are ways the world defines personal strength. But God's Word gives a paradoxical view of strength. Rest, quietness, and trust—these words all reflect a state of dependence.

Strength, at its core, is depending on God. Strength comes when we acknowledge our weakness and our need for God. When our sin overwhelms us, we repent and turn to Him for forgiveness. When we are weary of trying to earn His favor, we stop and remember we only have to receive His grace. In solitude, we hear Him speak and learn to pray. In getting to the end of our self-reliance, we trust Him for our needs. When we are willing to be emptied of self, then He can fill us with His life. 2 Corinthians 12:9 (NKJV) says, "And He said to me, 'My grace is sufficient for you, for My strength is made perfect in weakness.' Therefore most gladly I will rather boast in my infirmities, that the power of Christ may rest upon me."

What are the areas of your life where you need to depend more on God?

Father, remind me today that You are not asking me to be strong,
but to depend on You. In my weakness, You will be strong.
Help me to return, rest, listen, and trust. Amen.

....

....

....

....

....

....

....

LEAVE NO TRACE

*Whoever sows sparingly will also reap sparingly,
and whoever sows generously will also reap generously.*
2 CORINTHIANS 9:6 NIV

When you enter any state or national park, you will notice a recurring sign posted with a plea to hikers, climbers, campers, bicyclers, and horseback riders to leave no trace of their passing—no trash, no damaged vegetation, no fire rings, and so on. Where park visitors pass is to remain just as it was before—as if humans had never been there.

In our Christian lives, the "leave no trace" rule goes against all that Christ taught His disciples to do. The Christian's calling is to leave an imprint on all the lives we touch, sharing our relationship with Jesus through our words and actions.

There are unbelievers who have tried—and continue to try—to enforce a "no trace" rule upon Christians because they know the power of the gospel to change lives—even turn the political will of a whole country. But truth cannot be stopped.

The nature of Christianity is to bring others to salvation through the knowledge of Christ, sowing seeds of truth wherever possible. If a Christian passed through life without leaving a trace of their presence, then their life would be a tragic waste indeed.

*Dear Lord, I want to mark trails that will lead others to the wonder
of knowing You as Savior and friend. Help me not to waste my
life in laziness or in fear of telling others about You. Amen.*

....

....

....

....

....

....

PEACEFUL SLEEP

In peace I will both lie down and sleep,
for You alone, O Lord, make me to dwell in safety.
PSALM 4:8 NASB

Do you have trouble sleeping? Do you lie awake thinking, worrying about your future, or doubting your decisions? If this sounds familiar, you are normal. Welcome to the club! At some point in our lives, most women struggle with not being able to sleep at night.

The days are so hectic that often by the time you collapse into bed, your mind probably has not had time to settle down. It is still going a hundred miles an hour. Try reading the Psalms when you get into bed. Fill your mind and heart with God's Word. It will calm those worries that loop through your mind like a hamster on its wheel.

The Lord will bring you peaceful sleep. Say aloud to Him, "God, I know that I am safe with You. Give me a good night's sleep." He wants His precious daughter to rest in His care.

Lord, remind me to read the Bible before I go to bed at night
so that the last thoughts of the day are Your promises. Amen.

THE GREATEST OF THESE IS LOVE

And now these three remain: faith, hope and love.
But the greatest of these is love.
1 CORINTHIANS 13:13 NIV

Faith. . .hope. . .love. Without faith, it's impossible to please God. The truth is, it's often hard to look beyond our current circumstances and believe that all will turn out well. There are times our faith will be tested and tried. During these times, it's important to know what God's Word says about faith: "Now faith is the substance of things hoped for, the evidence of things not seen" (Hebrews 11:1 KJV).

Then there's hope. Are you hoping for something you're still waiting for? Remember, your hope is found in Jesus. He's your hope for a life full of happiness and love. He's your hope for a victorious life and, most important, your hope for an eternal future.

You may encounter times in life when your faith runs low. You may even feel you have no hope. But always know that nothing can ever separate you from the almighty love of God. His Word says that faith, hope, and love all remain, but the greatest of these is definitely God's love.

Dear God, help me to always share that same
unconditional love that You give me with others. Amen.

FINDING TIME TO
COMMUNE WITH GOD

*[Your words] will always be my most
prized possession and my source of joy.*

PSALM 119:111 CEV

Do you want to spend time with God but wonder how to fit it into your day? Ask God to give you creative ideas on ways to cultivate an intimate relationship with Him.

Linda lights a candle that reminds her to pray whenever she sees the flame. Elizabeth sets an alarm to beep when she needs to pray about a friend's doctor's appointment or other time-related prayer request. Brenda listens to Bible verses set to music.

Other ideas: Sign up for email prayer newsletters for your favorite ministries and pray over them before you check your personal email. Keep a Bible and devotional book in your purse so you can pray and study while waiting on appointments. Or write requests and Bible verses on index cards and tape them on your mirror and review them while you primp for the day. Why not pray while exercising, walking the dog, or performing other mundane tasks? And you could listen to audio devotionals and the Bible on CD while driving.

Above all, know that God desires for you to desire Him. If you ask Him to, He will help you create space for the things that will bring you closer to His heart.

*Father God, I love Your Word. Help me to make it a priority,
so we can get to know one another better. Amen.*

RED AS CRIMSON

*"Come now, let us settle the matter," says the LORD. "Though
your sins are like scarlet, they shall be as white as snow;
though they are red as crimson, they shall be like wool."*
ISAIAH 1:18 NIV

A woman entered a relationship with a Christian man with the best intentions. She never dreamed she would compromise herself in any way, but by the time the relationship ended, she'd stumbled in a major way. She couldn't forgive herself. Though she never admitted it to anyone, she secretly struggled with shame.

Have you ever walked in this woman's shoes? Found yourself falling. . .not just away from God, but away from the standards you felt certain were unshakable in your life? Did you struggle to forgive yourself after the fact?

It's often easier to forgive others for the things they've done to us than to forgive ourselves when we mess up. Thankfully, God stands ready to forgive. Today, if you have unconfessed sin in your life, take it to the One who longs to reason it out with you. Confess. . .and watch as those sins are washed whiter than snow. Then observe how your loving heavenly Father teaches you to forgive yourself.

*Lord, I come to You today, desperate for a clean slate. My sins
are red as crimson, but today I ask that You wash me clean.
Forgive me, Father, then teach me to forgive myself. Amen.*

CHOSEN FIRST

"I have chosen you," declares the LORD Almighty.
HAGGAI 2:23 NIV

Lydia felt like she was back in grade school waiting for one of the team captains to choose her for their kickball team. Who knew job hunting was going to be such a blow to her self-esteem? Silence from some potential employers coupled with immediate rejections from others left her discouraged and deflated.

Have you ever felt this way about a situation in your life? Whether it's a job hunt, a potential job promotion, a relationship, or something else, it's hard to deal with feeling like we're being overlooked or picked last.

God, in His loving plan, guaranteed your place in His family by picking you—first! Before you accepted His gift of grace, before you knew who God is, even before you were conceived, He chose *you*. He chose you, not as a nameless individual in a sea of faces, but as the person you uniquely are to Him. He loves you that much.

No position or promotion or relationship is as important as being handpicked by God for His team. Today, thank Him that He doesn't make us stand on the baseline kicking dust until He decides we're worthy enough to be on His team. And then get out there and play like the first pick that you are!

God, You know what it feels like to be rejected—to be overlooked.
Thank You for choosing me, even though I am unworthy of such
an honor. Help me to show Your love to others. Amen.

PROFESSING THE POWER OF PRAYER

I will consider all your works and
meditate on all your mighty deeds.
PSALM 77:12 NIV

Often, when we are faced with difficult situations, we ask close friends to pray for us. If we face a challenging situation at work, we ask people in our Bible-study classes to pray about it. If we are confronting an illness, we ask church leaders to pray for our healing. If we are struggling with a personal or spiritual issue, we ask a trusted prayer partner to pray and hold us accountable for our actions. Asking others to join us in praying about tough situations demonstrates that we believe God is faithful in answering prayers.

We also encourage people to believe in God's faithfulness when we report back on how He has met our needs. It encourages those who are facing a challenging work situation when we tell them how God set things right at work for us. When a friend is sick, we can encourage her by testifying to an instance when God healed us. If we know someone weighed down with a personal or spiritual issue, we can tell them how God delivered us in a time of need.

Asking for prayer and proclaiming God's faithful responses are essential ways in which we glorify Him and encourage each other.

Dear Lord, I praise You for the amazing works
You do. Bring to my mind specific great works
so I can focus on glorifying You for them. Amen.

PLANNING FOR THE FUTURE

Why, you do not even know what will happen tomorrow. What is your life?
You are a mist that appears for a little while and then vanishes. Instead,
you ought to say, "If it is the Lord's will, we will live and do this or that."

JAMES 4:14–15 NIV

It's hard not to look into the future and try to map out where life will take you.
Someone once said to go ahead and break out the fine china instead of living
with a paper-plate mentality! In other words, don't wait for a special occasion
or for your knight in shining armor to appear. Experience life to the fullest each
day you are given.

It's natural to plan for the future, to imagine that special relationship with a
man you hope will come along. God knows the desires of your heart, and He is
always interested in blessing you with the very best. It can be dangerous to our
hearts, however, to plot out our future without giving heed to God's Word.

James 4 warns us that we don't know how long this life will last. When we
make our plans, we should remember that our sovereign God holds each day in
His hands. Plan and pray within His will.

Father, remind me that You are sovereign. Teach me to remember
You as I make plans. I want Your will above all else. Amen.

A SONG IN THE NIGHT

*By day the LORD directs his love, at night his song
is with me—a prayer to the God of my life.*
PSALM 42:8 NIV

Have you ever thought of your life as being like a symphony? There are some high highs and some low lows. There are crescendo moments—where everything seems to fall into place, and there are some pianissimo moments, where things draw to a quiet stillness. And in the midst of it all, there is the Conductor, standing with baton in hand, directing. He calls the shots. He tells the musicians when to play furiously and when to slow to a halt.

God is the director of your life. During the daytime—when most of the major decisions of life are made—He's there, leading you, guiding you. And at night, when His direction might not be as clear, His song plays over you.

Today, begin to see your life as a symphony with many movements. Allow the Lord—your Conductor—to lead you through the highs and lows, the fortissimo moments and the pianissimo ones as well. Then when night shadows fall, listen closely for the song He's playing over you.

*Oh Father! I can almost hear the music now. Thank You for the reminder
that my life is a symphony and You are the Conductor. I don't want to
carry the baton, Lord. I willingly remove it from my hands. Direct me
in the daytime, and sing Your song over me at night. Amen.*

....

....

....

....

....

....

....

....

HOW DO YOU PICTURE GOD?

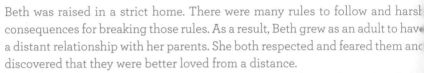

For we do not have a high priest who is unable to empathize
with our weaknesses, but we have one who has been tempted
in every way, just as we are—yet he did not sin.

<small>HEBREWS 4:15 NIV</small>

Beth was raised in a strict home. There were many rules to follow and harsh consequences for breaking those rules. As a result, Beth grew as an adult to have a distant relationship with her parents. She both respected and feared them and discovered that they were better loved from a distance.

Our parents provide an early template for our understanding of God. For those raised in loving and affectionate homes, the picture of God is one of love and security. But those who were raised in less-than-ideal environments have a more difficult time conceiving of a God who loves unconditionally. Thankfully, scripture paints a far more accurate picture of God than we can produce on our own. The Bible is filled with stories that illustrate God's character and His unconditional, boundless love for His children.

What does your picture of God look like? Is your template in line with what scripture says about Him? If you aren't sure, examine what God's Word says about His character. Take notice of how He interacts and communicates with biblical characters. Ask Him to open your heart and eyes so that you can see Him for whom He really is.

Father, I confess that at times my picture of You is
distorted. I pray You would reveal Yourself to me in
a fresh way so I see You for whom You are. Amen.

PRAISE ANOTHER, NOT YOURSELF

Let another praise you, and not your own mouth;
a stranger, and not your own lips.

PROVERBS 27:2 NASB

Sometimes when we women feel insecure, we try to make ourselves look good in a group. We may do this by spending too much money on name-brand clothing either to fit in or stand out as something special. We may attempt to lift ourselves up by boasting. We may drop names of important people into the conversation as if our association with them makes us better than others. We may tell of our accomplishments at work or even make mention of our good deeds in the community.

The Bible instructs us to find our worth in the knowledge that we are daughters of the King. We do not need to lift ourselves up by speaking highly of our works. In fact, in Proverbs, we are told not to praise ourselves with our own mouths.

Instead, find an opportunity to praise another person today. If there is a particular character trait that stands out to you in his or her life, acknowledge it verbally. You will find that in lifting others up, your heart is much more at peace than when you seek to elevate yourself.

God, show me someone today that I may honor. Remind me
I should not seek to bring attention to myself for my good
deeds but should do them for Your glory alone. Amen.

CHOCOLATE AND BROCCOLI

I want to do what is right, but I can't. I want to do what is good, but I don't.
I don't want to do what is wrong, but I do it anyway. But if I do what I don't want
to do, I am not really the one doing wrong; it is sin living in me that does it.

ROMANS 7:18–20 NLT

We women love our chocolate. Maybe if we consumed it only in pure cocoa form it would be good for us, but most of us love it with sugar and fat added and could eat it every day. Of course, our taste buds also may like broccoli, but unlike chocolate, we prefer it in small doses.

You might find yourself feasting daily on fears, worries, jealousies, and stress—the fat-laden chocolate of life. And just as we know we should eat good foods like broccoli, we know love, forgiveness, patience, and self-control are good for us, but most of us struggle to consume enough of them to keep our spiritual life healthy.

What we need is discipline in our spiritual (and physical) diet, but we can't do it on our own. We need God's power to help us crave those things that are the healthiest. Through prayer and biblical guidance, it is possible to change our taste buds to want what is best for our bodies and souls.

Lord, help me to feed my body and soul the things that will
keep me most healthy and useful to You. Help me to
crave the things that are best for me. Amen.

PLOTTING OR PRAYING

*Why do the nations conspire
and the peoples plot in vain?*
PSALM 2:1 NIV

Think for a minute about the intricacies of the human body. Consider all the involuntary functions the brain tells our bodies to carry on while we are conscious of only a few functions, like holding this book or reading this page.

Consider the many patterns and colors of nature and the cycles in which they occur. What about the complexity and beauty of various kinds of music and the ear that can hear them? Recall the myriad number of creatures and plants that live in the ocean. The Creator who made it is beyond our imagination. He is also beyond our control.

Why do we try to make our path without the all-powerful Creator God who does all things magnificently? Jeremiah 29:11 reminds us that God knows the plans He has for us, to give us a future and a hope. Wouldn't it be wiser to pray instead of plot?

Why not ask God what His plans are for your life? He knows the future, and He will lovingly lead you there. Pray first before planning. Ask Him. He will show you the way. With bowed head and bended knee, worship this One who spoke the world into being. And ask Him what plans you should make.

*Father, You made the world and all that is in it. You are the
author of past, present, and future. Forgive me for wasting much
time in vain plotting. Show me the plans You have for me. Amen.*

CREATIVITY

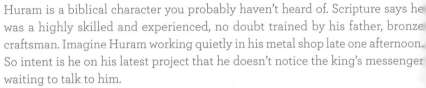

Huram was filled with wisdom, with understanding and with knowledge to do all kinds of bronze work. He came to King Solomon and did all the work assigned to him.

1 KINGS 7:14 NIV

Huram is a biblical character you probably haven't heard of. Scripture says he was a highly skilled and experienced, no doubt trained by his father, bronze craftsman. Imagine Huram working quietly in his metal shop late one afternoon. So intent is he on his latest project that he doesn't notice the king's messenger waiting to talk to him.

"Huram?" the man asks. "The king wants to see you."

Huram is confused. "Me? What on earth could he possibly want with me?" Huram must have wondered how an ordinary guy like him could be used in such an extraordinary way.

We see creativity throughout scripture. David wrote songs, Abraham built altars. The Israelites used their gifts of metalworking, sewing, and woodworking to build the Ark of the Covenant and God's temple.

God delights in creating and watching His children create with the gifts and abilities He has given them. What gifts, skills, and abilities has God given you? How can you use these things to honor Him?

Whether it's compiling and editing a newsletter for a local ministry, painting the walls of a friend's house, making meals for shut-ins, or sewing blankets for needy children, every gift and ability counts. Each time you find an opportunity to use your God-given talents and abilities, think about Huram and what an honor it is for ordinary people to serve God in extraordinary ways.

Father, help me to use my unique gifts
and abilities to serve You. Amen.

REDEMPTION

*Praise the Lord, my soul, and forget not all
his benefits. . .who redeems your life from the pit
and crowns you with love and compassion.*
PSALM 103:2, 4 NIV

You were in a pit. Not just clinging to the side, climbing your way out, almost to the top. You were deep down in the darkness of a pit with no escape route, no way out.

Whether you came to know Jesus at age nine or eighty-nine, you were not any closer to being able to save yourself. If your sins were many or few, it made no difference before a holy God. You were a sinner.

You needed a redeemer, a rescuer. You were desperate and doomed. You may have appeared to be alive, but in reality you were dead. Your soul was in darkness, longing for light. Your spirit was empty, longing to be filled.

And then you saw Him. You may have heard His name before, but it was nothing more than a name. You may have seen the cross, but it was just a symbol. This time was different. You realized you were lost without Him. You saw your situation for what it was. You were in a pit. You were stuck. You called out His name—"Jesus!"

Christ came down into the pit and lifted you up in His arms out of the muck and mire of disbelief. You were helpless, unable to save yourself. And then, simply by asking, by calling out for help, You were saved. He redeemed your life.

*Jesus, You lowered Yourself unto death to
redeem my soul. May I never forget. Amen.*

....

....

....

....

....

....

PERPETUAL COMMUNICATION

Listen to my prayer, O God, do not
ignore my plea; hear me and answer me.
My thoughts trouble me and I am distraught.

PSALM 55:1–2 NIV

For centuries, the handwritten letter was the main source of communication between friends separated by miles. Waiting for a reply could take several days or weeks.

With modern technology has come a revolution in how we communicate. We can exchange our thoughts with someone on the other side of the world in just a second or two. And we've become so enamored with communication that we now send notes, pictures, and our voice over a small device we carry everywhere.

So what does all this perpetual communication tell us about ourselves?

We want to be heard. We want to feel that others are listening to us and care about connecting with us. And we like to do it electronically.

But we have a significance that goes far beyond electronic wavelengths. God is tuning into our every little twitter of thought and activity, and He doesn't have to power up or log in to hear us.

Lord, thank You for hearing my cries for attention.
Help me to rest in knowing that my voice has significance
to You, and teach me to listen for Your replies. Amen.

CHASING THE WIND

*Enjoy what you have rather than desiring what
you don't have. Just dreaming about nice
things is meaningless—like chasing the wind.*
ECCLESIASTES 6:9 NLT

Modern-day women are inundated with marketing strategies. Every time we turn on the television, we're told what type of toothpaste we should use, what shampoo is best for our hair, and what jeans we should buy. And magazines are loaded with photos of the latest and greatest handbags, shoes, clothes, and makeup. Sometimes we get in the "To be my best, I have to *have* the best" mentality. We dream about all the things we wish we had, and even sacrifice to get them.

Chasing after the latest great "thing" is like chasing the wind. By the time you actually purchase the things you're longing for, trends will change. The winds will shift in a different direction.

What would it profit you to gain all the goodies and still lose your soul? Instead of dreaming about the things we don't have, we should be praising God for the things we do!

Lay your dreams at the Lord's feet. Think of the many ways He has blessed you, then begin to praise Him for the things you already have.

*Father, I'll admit I've chased after the wind at times.
I see pretty, trendy things and want them. Today, I hand
over my desires to You. Thank You for the many ways
You have already provided for me, Lord. Amen.*

SALVATION

But he was pierced for our transgressions, he was crushed for our iniquities;
the punishment that brought us peace was on him, and by his wounds we
are healed. We all, like sheep, have gone astray, each of us has turned to
our own way; and the LORD has laid on him the iniquity of us all.

ISAIAH 53:5–6 NIV

Pierced. Crushed. Punished. Wounded.

These are strong words. They are verbs of injury, hurt, and pain. As we read these verses in Isaiah, the words appear in black and white on a page. Not so the reality of the cross. Nails driven through hands and feet. A Roman soldier's sword through flesh. Sweat. Blood. A brow gouged and scraped by a crown of thorns, a crown of mockery.

It was not a neat and poetic paragraph as it sometimes appears to us as we read our leather-bound Bibles. Redeeming love was a day when the sun did not shine, when God turned His face from Jesus. It was excruciating suffering, torture, and death.

But that is only part of the story. It was a choice, a gift, a chance for all mankind to enter into a holy God's presence. Because of Christ's agonizing death, we may call God our *Father*, speak personally with the King, and one day walk the streets of heaven.

We must remember the price Jesus paid. God placed our sins upon His only Son. And that Son, that precious lover of our souls, accepted the mission.

By Christ's death, we have life.

Jesus, I am humbled. "Thank You" does not seem enough.
May my "thank You" be a life well-lived as a witness for You. Amen.

SHARING THE DEEP STUFF

*Gideon arrived just as a man
was telling a friend his dream.*
JUDGES 7:13 NIV

Do you have a special friend you can share your dreams with? Someone who knows the real you, the person deep down inside? If so, then you've found a real treasure.

Finding a kindred spirit is so important, especially for women. Knowing you have someone you can trust with your hopes, dreams, ideas, and failures makes you feel safe. And when you receive the validation of a close friend, you also receive the courage you need to step out and do what you've been called to do. True friends not only give us their stamp of approval, they invigorate us.

Consider something else from today's verse. Gideon arrived "just as" a man was telling a friend his dream. Has the Lord ever placed a godly friend in front of you "just as" you needed her?

There is a Friend you can trust above all others—the One who gave you those dreams in the first place. Talk about validation! He longs for you to confide in Him and to turn to Him with your deepest longings, as well as any hurt and pain. And He's always there. Talk about impeccable timing!

*Lord, thank You for planting dreams in my heart, and thank You
for giving me godly friends with whom to share those dreams.
Today, I praise You for the kindred spirits in my life. Amen.*

SOARING

But those who hope in the Lord will renew their strength.
They will soar on wings like eagles; they will run and
not grow weary, they will walk and not be faint.
ISAIAH 40:31 NIV

A runner will tell you that a good run is exhilarating. Some may jog a mile or so each morning, while others tackle marathons. No matter one's skill level or degree of stamina, every runner eventually tires. The human body simply cannot run forever with its own strength.

Are you weary? Some days you may find yourself pulled in many directions—work, family, church, and perhaps classes or raising children. You attempt to have some sort of a social life amid all the demands. You collapse at the end of each day.

Well, put on your sneakers because Isaiah 40:31 calls you a *runner*. In fact, this verse promises that you can soar! How is that possible, you may wonder? None of the responsibilities on your plate are going anywhere, and there remain merely twenty-four hours in a day.

In your own strength, there will be no running and certainly no soaring. That's why you need Jesus. Put your hope in Him. He promises to renew your strength. Marathon runners will never attain the ability to run and not grow weary, but you can. You are God's child, and He wants to see you soar.

God, I am weary from the demands of this life.
Help me to place just a tiny bit of hope, if that is all
I have today, in You. Renew my strength. I want to soar! Amen.

CHANGE YOUR MIND

*"Study this Book of Instruction continually. Meditate on it day
and night so you will be sure to obey everything written in it.
Only then will you prosper and succeed in all you do."*
JOSHUA 1:8 NLT

Cami had always been an optimistic and cheerful individual—until her car accident. When a teenager ran a red light and hit her car, Cami's confidence was greatly shaken. She became too anxious to drive, so she sought help from a qualified counselor. It took several weeks, but her counselor helped her learn practical steps for managing her anxiety, and Cami found that scripture spoke to her heart now in a way it never had prior to the accident. Gradually, as her thoughts transformed, Cami was able to drive again, and her cheerfulness and optimism returned.

Our thoughts influence our feelings and behaviors. In fact, our bodies physically respond to the things we think about. When we think negatively about ourselves or others, we are more likely to act on those thoughts. God designed our brains this way, which explains why scripture places such a high priority on maintaining our thought life. One of the most practical tools we have for improving it is to regularly meditate on scripture and commit it to memory. This discipline will literally transform our thoughts *and* our lives.

Father, help my thoughts be pleasing to You. Amen.

WAITING. . .FOR THE UNSEEN

But if we hope for that we see not,
then do we with patience wait for it.
ROMANS 8:25 KJV

Remember when you were a little girl and Christmas was coming? Maybe you hoped for a particular bicycle. You knew just what it looked like and could describe it perfectly. You waited with great anticipation for something you'd actually seen with your eyes. The image was crystal clear. And because you wanted it so badly, it was worth the wait.

It's one thing to wait on something you've seen, and it's another thing to wait on something you haven't. It's hard to get excited for something when you don't know what it looks like. And yet there are so many wonderful unseen things in our lives—blessings we haven't experienced yet. Jobs we haven't been given. Children who haven't been born. Relationships that haven't begun. Opportunities we haven't been offered. It's exciting to think of all the great things ahead.

Maybe you've been so stuck in the problems of the past that you can't see the future through hopeful eyes. Today, ask the Lord to renew your hope. The days ahead are filled with great adventure. . .and wonderful, unknown things. Oh, if only you could catch a glimpse! Then you would realize it's worth the wait.

Lord, sometimes I wish I could see what's coming.
There are so many things I have yet to see,
but I'm willing to wait, Lord. And while I wait,
please increase my hope and my patience. Amen.

RED SEA TRIALS

"The Lord will fight for you;
you need only to be still."
EXODUS 14:14 NIV

The Israelites found themselves in a terrifying predicament. The Red Sea was before them and the Egyptians were bearing down from behind. There was nowhere to go—no escape—no way out. They blamed Moses and questioned his judgment. In fear and desperation they cried out to the Lord for help. The Lord promised to fight for them as they demonstrated their trust by being still.

The Israelites' plight wasn't a surprise to the Lord. In fact, God brought them to that very place for His purposes. The Israelites would have to exercise their faith and trust Him to save them. The Egyptians would be destroyed when the parted waters engulfed them. The Lord would demonstrate His power and receive glory.

Have you ever encountered a Red Sea? Perhaps you felt hemmed in by life's circumstances. God is not taken by surprise. He allowed you to come to this place for certain reasons. Trust in the Lord with all your heart, and Satan will be destroyed as faith displaces fear. God will receive the glory. There is nothing we face that God cannot conquer. Be still. Know the Lord will fight for you. If God is for us, there is no one and no circumstance that can be against us.

Dear Lord, give me confidence in You when
I face Red Sea trials in life. As You made a way
for the Israelites, do the same for me. Amen.

....

....

....

....

....

....

....

THIS IS YOUR TIME

*"And who knows whether you have not
attained royalty for such a time as this?"*
ESTHER 4:14 NASB

To live in the center of God's will—to walk, step by step, the path He's prepared for us—is no easy task. At some point in our lives, we each wonder, *Why am I here? What did God make me to do?*

Too often we look for the big Hollywood blockbuster answer: *I will find a cure for cancer. I will solve world hunger. I will save thirty-eight children from a burning school bus.* While these things are possible, they're unlikely to happen to most of us.

Instead, God wants us to be sensitive to the opportunities He places in our lives—sometimes on a daily basis—to make a difference for His kingdom. Do you see someone who needs a good meal or just someone to talk to? Could you help out a coworker who is burdened with a heavy workload? Big or small, the choices we make to help others are just one part of the puzzle that is the meaning of life.

Like Queen Esther in the Old Testament, we need to examine our daily lives and consider. . .maybe God brought us to this very place for such a time as this.

*Father, please show me the purpose for my day today.
Open my eyes to the opportunities that You put before
me to make a difference in other peoples' lives. Amen.*

WITH GOD, ANYTHING IS POSSIBLE

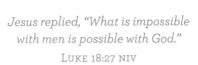

Jesus replied, "What is impossible
with men is possible with God."
LUKE 18:27 NIV

Have you ever lived through what appeared to be an impossible circumstance? Maybe it was starting over after a divorce, living through the loss of a loved one, surviving a devastating disease, or facing a mortgage payment when you knew the money just wasn't there.

Merriam-Webster defines the word *impossible* as "incapable of being, being done, or happening." As a Christian, you should know how Jesus defines the word. According to Luke 18:27, there are things that are impossible with men. But with God on your side, there is absolutely nothing that is impossible. No matter how difficult your problem may look, always remember God can turn impossibilities into possibilities.

Are you facing a situation that seems totally impossible? Friend, don't dwell on your problem or circumstance. Instead look only to God who makes all things possible. Put your complete trust in Him and His Word, and remove the word *impossible* from your vocabulary.

Dear God, I know there is nothing impossible
with You. I choose to put my complete trust
in You and Your Word. Amen.

THE WEE LITTLE MAN

*"For the Son of Man came to seek
and to save the lost."*
LUKE 19:10 NIV

Annette was never in the popular crowd back in high school, but she did try to be friends with just about everyone. That is, everyone except the cheerleaders. There was just something about those girls that screamed "insincere," and she had no desire to be a part of their fake little world. So several years later, when Kathryn, a former cheerleader, began working at the same company as Annette, Annette chose not to reconnect with her high school acquaintance. The problem was Kathryn happened to be in the midst of a painful divorce and really could have used Annette's friendship and encouragement.

Labels are often limiting, demeaning, and inaccurate. Zacchaeus understood the pain of a label. He was a tax collector. His peers had written him off as a thief and someone who definitely could not be trusted. As a result, there were probably very few people in Zacchaeus's world who were willing tell him about the love of Jesus. Thankfully, Jesus noticed Zacchaeus, because He never put people in a box. He loved them unconditionally.

Take a moment to consider the people around you. What limiting labels might you be placing on these souls? If Jesus lived in your home or worked in your office, how would He see these people? Is there a label that prevents you from connecting with someone who needs His love?

*Father, enable me to see people through Your eyes,
not through the limiting eyes of a label. Amen.*

SAY IT. . .DO IT!

When you make a vow to God, do not be late in paying it;
for He takes no delight in fools. Pay what you vow! It is better
that you should not vow than that you should vow and not pay.
ECCLESIASTES 5:4–5 NASB

Have you ever known people who made promises they didn't keep? Maybe they said they would call, but didn't. Perhaps they promised a lunch together or a movie, then simply got busy and forgot. It's frustrating, isn't it? A person like that is hard to trust. And when you have to work with someone who doesn't follow through, it can be even more frustrating.

How wonderful that God never forgets His promises. If He says it, He means it. And if He means it, He does it. Talk about keeping your word! God is the very epitome of trustworthiness.

Remember you are created in God's image, and He's all about honesty. So, pray before making commitments; then do what you've said you would. And when the Lord speaks into your life, giving you instruction—like ministering to someone in need or spending more time in the Word—get to it! Be a woman of your word—both to people and the Lord.

Lord, I want to be known as a woman of my word.
I want to be trustworthy. Today, remind me of the
commitments I've made, then set me back on the
right track to get those things done. Amen.

GOD HAS COMPASSION ON US

As a father has compassion on his children,
so the LORD has compassion on those who fear him.
PSALM 103:13 NIV

What does it mean that God has compassion on us? For some women, it means that God gives strength as they battle a chronic illness. For others, it means that He has forgotten their sins, because they came to Christ from a life of deep regrets.

Because we are all unique, God's compassion is individualized. Just as a father treats each of his children uniquely according to their ages and temperaments, so God deals with us as individuals.

How do you need God to show you His compassion today? Do you need guidance for a decision? Ask Him, and He will show you what to do. Perhaps you long for a companion to talk to. He is always available. Maybe you believe God couldn't love you because you've strayed from Him. Remember that He is the image of the loving father who ran to His prodigal son when he returned.

Another wonderful aspect of God's compassion is that once we've experienced it, we long to share it with others. So when you feel God has met your needs, ask Him how you can be a blessing to the people around you. Does a coworker need some encouragement? Or maybe your best friend could use some girl time. If you ask Him, God will give you fresh ideas on ministering compassion to those in your circle of influence.

Lord, I am so thankful for—and in awe of—Your compassion.
Help me spread it to everyone I know. Amen.

HIS WAITING, OUR WAITING

So the LORD must wait for you to come to him so he can
show you his love and compassion. For the LORD is a
faithful God. Blessed are those who wait for his help.
ISAIAH 30:18 NLT

Expectation is a big part of waiting. Planting and tending a garden yields a harvest. Pregnancy results in a baby. A letter brings news.

In the same way that we eagerly await happenings in our lives, God waits expectantly for us. He desires to be gracious to us; He longs to show us mercy. He uses time as His tool. He waits for opportunities to show kindness to us. Patiently, He leads us along, a shepherd with his flock, one step at a time.

As God waits for us, we also wait for Him. He is a God of goodness and justice. He loves us and He hears our cries. He will do what is right. Though we may have problems to face, He promises to be with us through them. He says He will never forsake us. To wait for Him is to expect Him to act, so be watchful. He will make Himself known to you. He says if we seek Him, we will find Him.

Anticipate His voice and leading. There is blessing for us in setting our focus on Him and waiting for His work in our lives.

Almighty God, thank You for Your mercy
and loving-kindness toward me, for waiting to be
gracious to me. Draw my attention to You and show
me how to watch and wait for Your goodness. Amen.

LISTENING TO GOD

Let the wise listen.
PROVERBS 1:5 NIV

For years Sheila saw herself as an ugly duckling. In fact, her mom had even said as much when she was growing up. Every time they read the children's story, her mother said, "Look Sheila, they wrote a story about you!"

Sheila carried this wound with her well into adulthood. Until one night she had a dream. In the dream a child was sitting on her father's lap. The father was speaking gently to the child, telling her over and over how beautiful and precious and unique she was. Sheila awoke from the dream in tears. She knew immediately God was speaking to her heart, and from that moment on she never again doubted her worth in His sight.

Has God ever spoken to you in a dream? There are many biblical accounts of God speaking to His children through dreams, and there is no reason why He wouldn't use this method today. This does not mean every dream is a message from God, nor that every dream contains deep spiritual meaning. Above all, meaning gleaned from dreams is never a substitute for biblical truth. But God can communicate with His children using any method He desires, and it is not surprising that He sometimes speaks to His children through dreams.

Whether you are awake or asleep, pray that God would open your eyes and your heart to whatever He wants to communicate to you.

Father, thank You for being the God of
all of me, even my dreams. Help me to
listen whenever You speak to me. Amen.

DON'T SAY IT

Do not let any unwholesome talk come out of your mouths,
but only what is helpful for building others up according
to their needs, that it may benefit those who listen.

EPHESIANS 4:29 NIV

The sequence of events is predictable: Random thoughts enter our minds; negative scenarios dominate our thinking; volatile emotions bubble up; before we know it, hurtful words come out of our mouths. We may not be able to control every thought that enters our minds, but the good news is we *can* control what thoughts we dwell on and what words we utter.

Learning to tame the tongue is a difficult task. First we must acknowledge the destruction our tongues are capable of. James 3 addresses the consequences of an unbridled tongue. Although our tongues are a tiny part of the body, they can do great harm to us, and others, if left unchecked.

Edifying speech begins with a disciplined mind. Weigh your thoughts against God's truth found in His Word. Dismiss lies. Yield your thought life to God's control. When God is allowed to guard our minds, our speech will be pleasing to Him and will truly benefit others.

Dear Lord, help me win the battle of the
tongue by dwelling on Your truth. Amen.

IRON-SHARPENING FRIENDSHIP

*Iron sharpeneth iron; so a man
sharpeneth the countenance of his friend.*
PROVERBS 27:17 KJV

Maybe you're familiar with the biblical expression "iron sharpens iron." But what does it mean? In order to keep things like knives sharp, they have to be rubbed against something equally as hard—something that can shape them into effective tools.

Godly friends will sharpen us. They won't let us grow dull in our relationship with God or others. They will keep us on our toes and work with the Lord to shape us into the most effective people we can be. Rubbing against them won't always be fun. In fact, we might feel the friction at times and wish we could run in the opposite direction. But don't run! Allow God to do the work He longs to do.

Take a good look at the friends God has placed in your life. Are there some who don't sharpen you? Perhaps you've been put in their lives to sharpen them. Are there a few who diligently participate in your life, growing you into a better, stronger person? Do they rub you the wrong way at times? Praise God! He's shaping and sharpening you into the person you are meant to be.

*Father, thank You for my friends, especially the ones who
keep me on my toes. Thank You for the sharpening work
You are doing in my life—even when it hurts! Amen.*

THANKSGIVING AS SACRIFICE

I am God Most High! The only sacrifice I want
is for you to be thankful and to keep your word.

PSALM 50:14 CEV

It's not difficult to say thank you. So why does the psalmist call thanksgiving a sacrifice? What are we giving up in order to be thankful? When we list our blessings, we realize we are recipients of many gifts—things God has given us freely, through no effort on our part.

Giving thanks is a means of letting go, of opening our hands and acknowledging God's power, control, and goodness. In the process, He frees us from ourselves. In the act of thanksgiving we are letting go of the control we think we have. We acknowledge once again that much of whom we are and what we have are gifts of a sovereign God who loves and blesses us. We sacrifice our pride and self-sufficiency when we say thank You.

Lord, give me a grateful heart. Cause me to turn
daily to You in thanksgiving and thus free myself
from pride and self-importance. Amen.

IT'S OKAY

*Make allowance for each other's faults
and forgive anyone who offends you. Remember,
the Lord forgave you, so you must forgive others.*
COLOSSIANS 3:13 NLT

Each of us has been hurt by another—with words spoken in anger, disastrous relationships, wounded hearts. We know God wants us to forgive one another, but how in the world is this accomplished? As fallen creatures, we prefer to keep score and tally up the wrongs against us. And why should we forgive unfair treatment? Because God's Word tells us to.

Paul states in Colossians that we must clothe ourselves in mercy, kindness, and patience. These qualities will make it easier to get over the hurt and pardon the grievance. He reminds us that the Lord forgave us, so we must forgive others. That's easier said than done, certainly. We need to focus on a person's worth, not their weaknesses, and turn our hearts to what can be, not what was.

An anonymous author wrote, "There's so much good in the worst of us and so much bad in the best of us, that we'll spend much of our lives learning to forgive and forget. Until you make the decision to forgive, the process of healing cannot begin." Releasing the grip we have on our anger will, in turn, release God's blessings.

*Dear heavenly Father, I know You command
us to forgive, but genuine forgiveness is difficult.
Help me to forgive those who have injured me. Amen.*

MOVING FORWARD

*Not that I have already obtained all this, or have
already arrived at my goal, but I press on to take
hold of that for which Christ Jesus took hold of me.*

PHILIPPIANS 3:12 NIV

Amy was a perfectionist. Whether she was working to get good grades, clean her apartment, or complete a work project, she spent countless hours tweaking, changing, and rearranging to be sure she attended to every minute detail. The problem was, no matter how hard Amy worked, she never felt successful. She eventually realized this mind-set was keeping her from accomplishing much of anything, since she was reluctant to start a project if she felt she couldn't do it perfectly.

This type of thinking can be very debilitating. We conclude that if we fail in one area, we are dismal failures. And that is a very accurate picture of what life was like under Old Testament law. Indeed, James 2:10 (NIV) says, "For whoever keeps the whole law and yet stumbles at just one point is guilty of breaking all of it." That's the bad news. The good news is we no longer live under the law. Romans 5:1–2 (NIV) says, "We have peace with God through our Lord Jesus Christ, through whom we have gained access by faith into this grace in which we now stand."

Now we live under grace. Grace frees us from the bondage of perfection. Praise God for His gift of grace.

*Father, thank You that I can be done with being
a perfectionist since I am under grace. Amen.*

....

....

....

....

....

....

SET APART FOR HIM

You can be sure of this: The LORD set apart the godly
for himself. The LORD will answer when I call to him.

PSALM 4:3 NLT

Doesn't it make you feel special to know you are called, chosen, and set apart to do great things for God? And while the Lord doesn't play favorites, He does have a way of making you feel pretty special. You are dearly loved—one of His little darlings. And His ear is always tuned into your heart. That's pretty amazing, isn't it? Parents always know the voices of their children, and God is no different. He hears your every cry, even before you make it!

Today, ponder the realization that you've been set apart. What does that mean to you, and how does it affect your walk with God? Does it change the way you view Him? Does it put a spring in your step? Make you feel like curling up with Him for a long chat?

God desires an intimate relationship with you. That's why you've been set apart—to be with Him. Take full advantage of that! Head to your prayer closet and let the Lord share His heart with you. Then open your heart and share it with Him, as well.

Lord, I feel so special knowing You've set me apart
for Yourself. I long for an intimate relationship with
You and gladly come into Your throne room for
some serious one-on-one time today. Amen.

THE SABBATH

*"Remember the Sabbath
day by keeping it holy."*
EXODUS 20:8 NIV

Remembering the Sabbath is not something God takes lightly. It is included in the Ten Commandments. Keeping the Sabbath holy goes back to Genesis. God made the world in six days. He worked. He created. He delighted in His masterpieces—the ocean, land, trees, flowers, and animals of all types. Best of all, He made man and woman in His own likeness. On the seventh day work ceased, and God rested.

Work is a good thing. After all, God created it. And there are many warnings in His Word against idleness. God takes work seriously. We are to work for six days and rest on the Sabbath. We are to keep the Sabbath day holy. It is meant for rest.

Many of us worship with other believers on Sunday but don't really rest throughout the remainder of the day. Take this challenge. For one month, strive to keep the fourth commandment. Keep the Sabbath holy. Don't clean your home, wash your car, or break out the laptop to complete that project you'd like to submit on Monday morning. Rest. Meditate upon the Lord. Relax. Take it easy. What a great commandment!

The book of Exodus tells us the Lord blessed the Sabbath and made it holy. You will find great blessing as you set apart this one day each week for rest.

*God, in this busy world, often Sunday
becomes just another day. Help me to
keep it holy as You have commanded. Amen.*

WHAT IS YOUR ISAAC?

Abraham built an altar there and arranged the wood on it. He bound his son Isaac and laid him on the altar, on top of the wood. Then he reached out his hand and took the knife to slay his son. But the angel of the LORD called out to him from heaven "Abraham! Abraham!" "Here I am," he replied. "Do not lay a hand on the boy," he said. "Do not do anything to him. Now I know that you fear God, because you have not withheld from me your son, your only son."

GENESIS 22:9–12 NIV

God asked Abraham to sacrifice his only son. Isaac had been born to Abraham and his wife, Sarah, in their old age and was very special to his father. Yet Genesis tells us Abraham did not hesitate when God asked him to make this enormous sacrifice. He rose early the next morning and took Isaac to the mountaintop.

Abraham would not withhold even his precious son from the Lord. He didn't understand God's request, and certainly his hand must have been shaking as he raised the knife. Nonetheless, he was willing. His answer was yes.

What is your Isaac? What would be hard to lay upon the altar if God called you to give it up? Is it your job or reputation, a relationship, or a dream? Often the Lord just wants to know that following Him is number one in your life—no matter the cost.

Lord, search my heart. Is there something I need to give up so that I might follow You more closely? Amen.

SECURE YOUR OWN MASK FIRST

Keep a close watch on how you live and on your teaching. Stay true to what is right for the sake of your own salvation and the salvation of those who hear you.
1 TIMOTHY 4:16 NLT

Why is it people in churches and other groups where volunteers are essential seem to believe that single, childless women have all the time in the world to get work done?

Every woman needs to guard her time wisely—whether single or married. We are all in danger of getting exhausted running here and there to do all the things that are seemingly good and intended to bring glory to God.

So before agreeing to take on a volunteer position, recall how flight attendants remind airline passengers in the event of emergency to secure their own oxygen masks before helping others around them. In many ways God tries to tell us this also as He reminds us not to neglect our time in prayer, study, and fellowship with Him. If our spiritual oxygen isn't flowing from a full tank, our ability to assist others will run out and we'll become useless.

Securing our own mask first sometimes means saying "no" to groups that see us as "singularly" available and "yes" to God who truly requires our time. Only then will we be alert and equipped to serve others in His strength.

Dear Lord, help me to prioritize my schedule so I can be refreshed and energized by time with You and in turn be inspired to do the tasks You place before me. Amen.

I LOVE YOU. . .EVEN
IN THE HARD TIMES

A friend loveth at all times.
PROVERBS 17:17 KJV

A woman walked her best friend through a difficult season. Health problems, a death in the family, and a serious bout with depression threatened to be her friend's undoing. Still, the woman stuck with it. Even when her friend insisted she didn't want anyone around. *Especially* when her friend insisted she didn't want anyone around.

Have you ever walked a friend though a tough season? Been there when she faced depression or pain? Held her hand as she mourned the loss of someone she loved? Walked with her through an illness or job-related challenge? Cried with her as her marriage came to a painful end? If so, then you truly know what it means to love at all times. Friendship—true friendship—runs deeper than the unexpected challenges of life.

Today, think of a friend who is going through a particularly difficult season. What can you do to lift her spirits? How can you encourage her to keep going? Should you send a card? Flowers? Make a phone call? Write an encouraging note? Take her to see a movie? Remember: God-breathed love pours itself out at all times.

Lord, I want to be a blessing to my friends who are hurting,
to show my love at all times. Today I recommit myself to
caring for my friends, especially during the difficult times.
Give me Your heart and show me what I can do to lift
my friend's spirits when she's down. Amen.

YES, LORD, YES, LORD, AMEN

"The joy of the LORD is your strength."
NEHEMIAH 8:10 NIV

In our success-driven world, fun is an often-overlooked commodity. There's a corporate ladder to climb, a glass ceiling to break through, another committee meeting to attend. Serious, staid, and structured, our lives lack joy. We race a ticking clock with a sweep hand.

Paul exhorted the Christian community to be full of joy *now*. The Psalms encourage us to sing and dance and praise His name. How is that possible with a solemn face? A little lighthearted fun releases pent-up tension and balances life's scales. Laughter will lower our blood pressure. That cheerful heart is good medicine.

Surely it's time for a bit of spontaneity. 1 Thessalonians 5:16 (NIV) says to "be joyful always." In our cyberspace world, we can share jokes and hilarious videos. Pull one up on the screen, throw back your head, and laugh. Realize God intended for us to have joy in our lives. Say, "Yes Lord," and chuckle.

Father, I live in a world loaded with danger, serious issues,
and worry. Help me to find joy in my life this day. Amen.

WHAT TO WEAR

*Therefore, as God's chosen people, holy and
dearly loved, clothe yourselves with compassion,
kindness, humility, gentleness and patience.*
COLOSSIANS 3:12 NIV

We all spend time selecting what to wear each day. Sometimes it is simply a matter of what is clean (or can at least be resurrected from the dirty clothes hamper!)

Some women are trendy, which requires them to keep up with the latest fashions. Others are more practical as they piece together a week's worth of outfits with just a couple pairs of neutral-colored pants and some solid-colored tops.

Clothing is important. It says something about a person. Think about black-tie affair, interview, tennis match, or day on the beach. Each calls for different type of attire. To show up on the beach in a tuxedo or at the tennis match in a business suit would be ridiculous!

As believers, God tells us to clothe ourselves with compassion, kindness, humility, gentleness, and patience. These traits cannot be found in a department store or in the latest fashion magazine. They can only come from the Holy Spirit living in and through us.

Today as you choose the clothing you will wear, choose also to clothe yourself with godly characteristics that will cause you to shine as a daughter of the Lord.

God, it is not always easy to be kind or compassionate. Sometimes humility, gentleness, and especially patience, are also difficult. Help me to be certain I am fully clothed with these attitudes before I leave home each morning. Amen.

A HOLY PERFUME

*For we are a fragrance of Christ to God among those
who are being saved and among those who are
perishing; to the one an aroma from death to death,
to the other an aroma from life to life.*

2 Corinthians 2:15–16 NASB

mells are all around us. The aroma of lavender relaxes us, the scent of coffee
imp-starts us, and the odor of a skunk offends us.

Have you ever considered how a person's spirit has an aroma? When you
neet someone who is godly, gentle, and sincerely kind, their spirit seems to
xude an inviting aroma like home-baked cookies or mulled apple cider that
.raws others in. But there are also people you meet who almost immediately
eem to give off a sharp odor like vinegar or ammonia. They have an unsettled
pirit in which bitterness and discontent are cultivated.

What kind of scent do you want your spirit to emanate? Remember that it
as the power to change a room and even a whole community.

As you perform your daily hygiene, putting perfume on your skin, consider
lso your spiritual perfume. Keep the scent fresh, not overpowering, and welcoming
y keeping your spirit in line with the Spirit of God through prayer, Bible study,
nd praise.

*Holy Spirit, I welcome You into my life. Be a perfume
that proves to others that You are sovereign in my life
and that draws them to Jesus Christ. Amen.*

SUCH AS THESE

People were bringing little children to Jesus for him to place his hands on them, but the disciples rebuked them. When Jesus saw this, he was indignant. He said to them, "Let the little children come to me, and do not hinder them, for the kingdom of God belongs to such as these."

MARK 10:13-14 NIV

Have you ever watched children worship? They do it with abandon. They're no restricted by the "I wonder if people are watching me?" question. In fact, the never even think about it. When the music begins, they just begin to celebrate with pure hearts and no hidden motivations or agendas.

Jesus longs for us to come to Him as children. To give up worrying about what others think and to simply come with a pure heart, ready to worship. You might have to shake off some worries and fears, and you might have to abandon your traditional way of approaching Him, but it will be worth it.

Take a look at today's scripture. When the disciples tried to send the children away—thinking they were annoying Jesus—He stopped them in their tracks. *"Do not hinder them. The kingdom of heaven belongs to such as these."* Makes you want to have a childlike faith, doesn't it? Come to Him—on every occasion—as a child.

Lord, please restore my childlike faith today.
Help me overcome any insecurities and simply
come to You with unbridled affection. Amen.

VALUING PEOPLE OVER THINGS

*Then Mary took about a pint of pure nard,
an expensive perfume; she poured it on
Jesus' feet and wiped his feet with her hair.*

JOHN 12:3 NIV

Mary and Martha must have felt especially grateful to have Jesus over for dinner. Only recently had He raised their brother Lazarus from the dead. They couldn't believe Lazarus was still with them, or that their beloved Jesus was in their home for another meal.

To her guests' surprise, Mary took a pint of luxurious perfume and washed Jesus' feet with it. As if that weren't shocking enough, she stooped to wipe His feet with her hair. As the scent of perfume and the outrageousness of Mary's act wafted through the air, Judas jumped up from the table in indignation.

"This should have been sold! We should have given the money to the poor!"

Perhaps Judas was acting out of nervous energy—he was about to betray Jesus to the authorities. Or maybe he was trying to feel better about himself by pointing out Mary's wastefulness. But as always, Jesus saw through Judas' actions right to his heart. He acknowledged the truth of Judas' heart (Jesus knew Judas had been stealing), while acknowledging the purity of Mary's actions (she was symbolically preparing Him for burial).

Jesus valued people over things. He considered the person's heart to be more important than their actions or outward appearance. What do you value?

Father, help me to value the things that You do. Amen.

FIT TOGETHER

*He makes the whole body fit together perfectly. As each part
does its own special work, it helps the other parts grow, so that
the whole body is healthy and growing and full of love.*

<small>EPHESIANS 4:16 NLT</small>

Have you ever put together a really large jigsaw puzzle? Maybe you struggled to get all of the pieces to fit in place. Some were obvious, others were a challenge.

The body of Christ is a lot like a giant puzzle. It's filled with many, many pieces, and they all fit together seamlessly to form the most beautiful picture on earth—more beautiful than any seascape or mountain peak.

Each piece in a puzzle is critical to the whole. Sure, when you look at them individually, you might wonder, "How in the world can this piece fit? It doesn't look like any of the others. It's not shaped like any of the others." Still, it fits! And when you see it in its proper place, it makes perfect sense.

This is a great day to praise the Lord for the many puzzle pieces—Christian brothers and sisters—you've been given. Think about the ones in the farthest reaches of the earth. They're all a part of this glorious picture that makes up the church.

*Oh Lord, I'm so grateful that everyone in the body of Christ has
a place. Thank You for fitting us together so beautifully. And thank
You that we've each been given our own job to do. May I learn to
do mine well, so that others might grow in You. Amen.*

More Editions of
3-Minute Devotions for Women

3-Minute Devotions for Women—Large Print

This devotional packs a powerful dose of comfort, encouragement, and inspiration into just-right-sized readings for women on the go. Each day's reading meets women right where they are—and is complemented by a relevant scripture and prayer.

Paperback / 978-1-68322-609-3 / $7.99

3-Minute Devotions from the Psalms: Inspiration for Women

This devotional delivers a powerful message of comfort, reassurance, and inspiration from the Psalms into just-right-sized readings for busy women. Each day's reading meets readers right where they are—and is complemented by a relevant scripture and prayer.

Paperback / 978-1-68322-400-6 / $4.99